The Trust Factor
Strategies for School Leaders

Julie Peterson Combs, Stacey Edmonson,
and Sandra Harris

EYE ON EDUCATION
6 DEPOT WAY WEST, SUITE 106
LARCHMONT, NY 10538
(914) 833–0551
(914) 833–0761 fax
www.eyeoneducation.com

Library of Congress Cataloging-in-Publication Data

Combs, Julie, 1955-
    The trust factor : strategies for school leaders / by Julie Peterson Combs, Stacey
Edmonson, and Sandy Harris.
        pages cm
    Includes bibliographical references.
    ISBN 978-1-59667-241-3
1. Educational leadership—United States. 2. Educational leadership—Moral and
ethical aspects—United States. 3. School management and organization—Moral and
ethical aspects—United States. 4. Trust. I. Edmonson, Stacey. II. Harris, Sandra, 1946–
III. Title.
    LB2806.C554 2013
    371.2—dc23
                                                                2013000978

10 9 8 7 6 5 4 3 2 1

Sponsoring Editor: Robert Sickles
Production Editors: Lauren Beebe and Lauren Davis
Copyeditor: Sarah Chassé
Designer and Compositor: Bruce Leckie
Cover Designer: Knoll Gilbert

ACKNOWLEDGMENTS

The ideas in this book originated from our conversations with educators and from our experiences in schools as leaders and followers. In general, as followers, we decide to trust a leader to the extent that the leader will care for our interests. When the leader demonstrates care, concern, and competency, we learn about trust. When the leader acts in ways that are dishonest, disrespectful, and harmful, we learn about distrust. Our capacity to write this book is somewhat based on the leaders we have followed in our lives and their actions related to building and breaking trust. We want to acknowledge all of these leaders, including our parents, our teachers, and our administrators. Much of our experiential knowledge about trust began with our interactions with these people, and we sincerely thank each of them. We dedicate our book to them, and we thank them for building trusting environments that nurture and support students, teachers, and coworkers.

We feel fortunate that early in our careers, a few mentors showed us effective and trustworthy leadership. In particular, Julie would like to recognize Dr. Debra Nelson. Debra, who has dedicated her career to public-school children, continues to demonstrate what trust in leadership looks like. Besides being kind, compassionate, and competent, she handles difficult situations with grace and a sense of humor. Most importantly, she possesses a faith and belief in others such that they want to rise to the highest of standards. Debra is a model of the positive strategies that we have described, and her influence will continue for years to come.

Many individuals helped us finalize the ideas in this book. In the formative stages, we want to thank the following teachers and school leaders for sharing their thoughts about trust and leadership: Lisa, Don, Andra, Donna, Sharon, Jan, Crickett, Lori, Carol, Lillian, Allison, and Susan. In addition, a special thanks to all the anonymous reviewers, along with their suggestions, that made this a better book. Thank you to Bob Sickles, president at Eye On Education, for his personal words of encouragement. Bob is a remarkable leader and visionary in education. The talented staff at Eye On Education, including our editors, Lauren Beebe and Lauren Davis, deserve much praise for bringing our ideas into the final production of the book.

We thank the team of friends and colleagues who have encouraged us throughout this process. These supporters continue to provide an ongoing dialogue about trust in our organizations. In particular, we offer our appreciation to Rebecca, Susan, and Keith for their feedback and encouragement. Finally, we want to recognize our many family members and especially our children, who have continued to support our work as teachers and leaders. Thank you to Christian, Kevin, Gregory, Andrew, Abigail, and Jamey.

MEET THE AUTHORS

Julie Peterson Combs is associate professor of educational leadership at Sam Houston State University. Previously, she worked as a school principal for ten years. She currently serves as the director of the doctoral program in educational leadership, where she teaches academic writing and research methods to doctoral students, along with leadership courses in the principal certification program. In addition to maintaining an active research agenda focused on stress and coping, academic writing, and the role of the school principal, she has written more than fifty journal articles, six book chapters, and coauthored two other books: *Managing Conflict: 50 Strategies for School Leaders* and *Examining What We Do to Improve Our Schools: 8 Steps from Analysis to Action*.

Stacey Edmonson is professor of educational leadership at Sam Houston State University in Huntsville, Texas, where she teaches courses in qualitative research, current issues, ethics, and school law. Formerly, she has been a central office administrator, principal, and teacher in Texas public schools. Her research interests include stress and burnout among educators, legal issues in education, and educator ethics. She has authored a number of books and articles and presents at regional, state, and national conferences on these and other related topics, in addition to consulting with school districts.

Sandra Harris is currently professor and dissertation coordinator at the Center for Doctoral Studies in Educational Leadership at Lamar University in Beaumont, Texas. Formerly she served as a teacher, principal, and superintendent in public and private schools. Her scholarship agenda includes administrator preparation and building relationship-oriented, socially just school environments. She presents at regional, state, and national conferences on these and other leadership-related topics. She has authored or coauthored twenty books, including *BRAVO Teacher!, BRAVO Principal!,* and *Managing Conflict: 50 Strategies for School Leaders* for Eye On Education.

SUPPLEMENTAL DOWNLOADS

The tools in this book are also available on Eye On Education's website as Adobe Acrobat files. Permission has been granted to purchasers of this book to download these resources and print them.

You can access these downloads by visiting Eye On Education's website: www. eyeoneducation.com. From the home page, click on FREE, then click on Supplemental Downloads. Alternatively, you can search or browse our website to find this book, then click on "Log in to Access Supplemental Downloads."

Your book-buyer access code is TTF-7241-3.

Index of Supplemental Downloads

TABLE OF CONTENTS

INTRODUCTION

Trust makes the difference between leaders who succeed and leaders who do not. As former school leaders, we base this assertion on our experiences. Now, as educational researchers, we have witnessed the accumulation of research findings within the past decade confirming the premise that trust matters. Because we believe that trust is an essential resource for school improvement, we are sharing our thoughts in this book. We have written this book for you—teachers, principals, assistant principals, central office personnel, superintendents—educational leaders who care, who are learners, and who are dedicated to personal and organizational effectiveness.

What Is Trust?

If someone asked you, "What exactly do you mean by trust?" you might struggle to find the words. Instead of words, consider a metaphor shared by Stephen Covey (2004) several years ago. Relationships can be like bank accounts that we have with one another; we make trust deposits (trust builders) and trust withdrawals (trust busters) with our actions and words. Some of our trust accounts can be in the red and overdrawn, meaning that we have a trust deficit. Trust withdrawals can happen when we share confidential information, have bouts of anger, blame others, or take the credit for the work of others, to name a few examples. We make trust deposits when we are open, honest, reliable, consistent, and encouraging. As leaders, we maintain individual accounts with hundreds of people, such as students and teachers. When we have high trust with others, trust acts as an insulator for many problems. For example, when we make mistakes as leaders, people who trust us are more forgiving and benevolent in their reactions.

People who work in high-trust organizations often take trust for granted. As we attempt to understand trust, identifying the opposite or conditions that signal low trust can be helpful. In low-trust organizations, the following behaviors have been documented by researchers:

- Individuals question the intentions of others.
- Individuals are reluctant to share and to be open with one another.
- Over time, people do only the minimum amount of work.
- In meetings, individuals passively listen and appear uninvolved.
- Small groups of teachers led by informal leaders meet to attempt to "save" the school.
- People do not feel emotionally safe; many teachers withdraw into their classrooms and "shut the doors."
- Leaders tend to fixate on small, unimportant problems.

Although many books have been written about trust for business leaders, we believe that school leaders have different contexts and different needs. A study by Anthony Bryk and Barbara Schneider (2002) presented compelling evidence that trust in schools is a strong predictor of student achievement, even stronger than socioeconomic status. Moreover, teachers participating in this study defined trustworthy building leaders as those who were competent, reliable, fair, open, and authentic. Bryk and Schneider described that trust was built and sustained in the highest-performing schools when teachers, parents, and school leaders made sense of their work together. One goal of this book is to help leaders make sense of their roles in facilitating trust in their schools.

Who Should Read This Book?

Specifically, we have written this book for the following leaders:

1. SCHOOL LEADERS IN NEW ROLES. School leaders with new assignments and positions face countless challenges. At the core of many of these challenges is the ability to establish and to sustain trusting relationships with teachers, students, and the community. We have seen many new leaders struggle because they underestimated the importance of trust. Some of these new leaders experienced marginal, if any, success because they could not earn the trust of their communities within the first eighteen months, which is considered the critical period to establish trust in new situations.

2. LEADERS EXPERIENCING CHANGE. School leaders accept challenging positions that come with high expectations for change and student success. Given these high expectations and the focus on improvement, many leaders have underestimated the power of trusting relationships in the change process. We have concluded that many well-intentioned leaders are simply unaware. They do not recognize their actions and words that destroy trust, nor do they understand the signs of pervasive low trust in an organization. Further, they do not have strategies to address low-trust issues, which can be very difficult to amend.

3. EDUCATIONAL LEADERS IN GENERAL. For leaders at all levels, developing trust can be challenging because of the nature of the supervisory position, which often creates a mentality of "us" versus "them." Educational leaders are expected to evaluate, discipline, and terminate employees. Even though these responsibilities can compromise trust, we believe that trust is still possible. As such, this book is written to help leaders at all levels recognize how their words and actions can destroy trust or how their words and actions can build and sustain trust with others.

How This Book Is Organized

Because we understand that school leaders are very busy people, we have presented the trust concepts in brief, easy-to-read chapters. Although the book can be read from beginning to end, we have designed it to be read in any order. In addition, we envision leaders using the book as a reference with a specific problem in mind.

The book is organized into three sections: Trust Busters, Trust Builders, and Trust Boosters. We begin by describing some common attitudes of school leaders that essentially destroy trust. We offer these fifteen trust busters so leaders can identify attitudes or behaviors that harm trust. Realizing that we all have shortcomings with trust, we conclude each trust buster with suggestions on how to eliminate these behaviors and attitudes. Following the trust busters are twenty-five essential trust builders for leaders. These strategies do not work in isolation, but together they help leaders develop trust. In the third section, we present ten trust boosters that can help leaders expand upon some of the basic trust concepts presented in the first two sections of the book. Finally, assessment tools for each section are provided as a way for leaders to review all the concepts in the section and to pinpoint strengths and areas for growth.

Because we believe that the reader of this book wants to lead well and wants to improve, we conclude each chapter with a list of questions in the section For Further Reflection. Self-reflection is the first step in meaningful change at both the personal and organizational levels. As such, this book is designed to invoke self-reflection, which truly is the only way that individuals can increase their trustworthy behaviors and ultimately improve the relationships in their schools.

Conclusions

The ability to model and maintain trusting relationships is a critical leadership skill. High trust provides the platform for change and innovation. Conversely, distrust leads to the disengagement of dedicated, talented educators. A newly appointed leader has a window of opportunity, during which actions and words will soon form the perceptions of character. Given that organizations can be polluted with duplicity, apathy, and distrust, in this book we offer information that will allow leaders to assess their own levels of trust and then proactively build and boost their trust levels with others.

PART I

Trust Busters

Trust busters happen. We all make mistakes. Sometimes we are
misunderstood, sometimes we make bad decisions, and sometimes
we have not yet learned needed strategies. Regardless, we do things
and say things as leaders that lead to trust withdrawals. What matters is how we address these busters. We have chosen fifteen of these
trust busters to appear first in the book because they represent some
common attitudes and actions that are often barriers to building
trust with others. At the end of each trust buster, we offer several
suggestions for the leader to eliminate trust-eroding habits and work
toward building trust.

TRUST BUSTER

"I Want Your Input, But Not Really"

You have a right to your opinions. I just don't want to hear them.

—Anonymous

How a leader makes decisions can be a trust buster or a trust builder. However, many times, leaders involve faculty and staff in what we call *pseudo–decision making*. Pseudo–decision making happens when individuals give time and energy to decisions that have been already made. Following are some common problems we have observed with decision making in organizations:

THE DECISION HAS BEEN MADE. The leader manipulates others to participate in decisions when the decisions have already been made. Sometimes leaders think that they can develop support for a decision, so they involve others in this contrived process. However, people will eventually see the deception and feel angry that their time was wasted. Trust will be broken, and individuals will be reluctant to invest time in the future.

DECISIONS ARE TOP-DOWN. When decision making is generally a top-down model, groups or individuals typically are reluctant to share differing ideas because of intimidation and fear, both symptoms of low-trust organizations. Additionally, there is a feeling of annoyance if faculty are required to attend meetings or to complete surveys to assist in providing feedback when there is consistent evidence that the decision will be made at the top. Creativity declines; dissention and unrest increase.

DECISIONS HAVE TO BE UNANIMOUS. Valuable time and energy are wasted when leaders seek unanimous decisions. The problem with unanimous decisions (i.e., complete agreement) is that these decisions sometimes indicate real problems with trust in the organization. One reason is that unanimous decisions often have characteristics of groupthink. The practice of groupthink leads to stagnation and decline within an organization because members value harmony and agreement such that opposing ideas are unwelcome.

DECISION AUTHORITY IS UNCLEAR. Sometimes, leaders do not have authority to make certain decisions in their schools; however, they continue to involve others in meetings to get feedback that is never used. The input of the faculty and staff is called upon, but in reality, their input is neither wanted nor considered.

So what actions can leaders take to change these trust-busting pseudo-decision-making behaviors? Here are some suggestions:

- Commit to not involving others in decision making unless their input is needed, valued, and will be used in some fashion.
- If a decision has already been made (and sometimes this is necessary), communicate this action clearly to others. When possible, provide a rationale so that others have some knowledge of how and why the decision was made. This rationale can increase trust and eventual support from others.
- Remember that unanimous decisions are rare. After all, it is almost impossible to have 100 percent agreement with everyone about anything. As Aesop said: "Please all, and you will please none." Try, instead, to work toward consensus. (For more information, see Trust Builder #18: Build Consensus.)

- Do not manipulate others. Involve them in the process when their involvement is wanted and needed, but do not manipulate them to think they are participating in a decision that has already been made.
- Consider using a strategy such as nominal group technique (NGT), which is a structured method for obtaining group input. NGT is conducted in a way that allows ideas and suggestions to be made anonymously. For more information on NGT, see www.creatingminds.org/tools/ngt.htm.

Involve others only when you need or want their input. If you do not intend to use others' ideas, then do not involve them in the process for that particular decision. How leaders involve others in making decisions in their schools is an important opportunity for trust building.

For Further Reflection

1. When was the last time you were manipulated to think that you were participating in decision making? How did that affect your trust levels with the leaders?
2. Site-based management is a practice that encourages participation in decision making. What topics could allow for group decision making (e.g., budgeting, staffing, school climate, curriculum, student achievement)?
3. Identify what strategies you use to get thorough, creative input from faculty and staff members.
4. When seeking input regarding decisions at your school, how do you respond when a suggestion is not one that you prefer?

Remember

Pseudo–decision making is a trust buster because leaders obtain others' input and then do not consider it in decision making. This type of decision making frustrates people and wastes their time.

"I Ignore Incompetence"

All problems become smaller if you don't dodge them,
but confront them.
—WILLIAM F. HALSEY JR.

Have you worked for someone who was really nice and friendly but also a pushover? Perhaps this individual had difficulty saying no. When presented with problems, maybe he was like the ostrich and stuck his head in the sand. Or maybe he recognized problems but was too busy or afraid to address them with individuals. If you have worked with a leader like this, you recognize this behavior as a trust buster.

Competence has been identified by researchers as one important component of the trust relationships in schools. Specifically, leaders who lack competence and allow others to remain incompetent break trust. Even leaders who intentionally try to build or repair trust will have a difficult time if they ignore incompetence. Ignoring the incompetence of others is like the proverbial wisdom that their actions will speak much louder than their words.

When managing others, competent leaders set the expectations. Then, the expectations are reviewed and modeled. When an employee does not follow the expectations, the leader should identify those specific behaviors. Together, the leader and the employee should discuss plans for improvement, make commitments to action, and provide formative feedback on progress. Finally, competent leaders provide the support, resources, and supervision to address and remedy performance concerns.

Too often ineffective leaders do not have the courage to address incompetence, and, as a result, they allow trust to be eroded in the work environment. Even though the conversations will be difficult, the *trust-building* leader understands the impact of allowing incompetence to continue. Leaders who ignore incompetence are not serving in the vital role of being an advocate for students. This trust-busting behavior puts the needs of the adults (including the leader, to avoid difficulty) above those of the students. Ignoring incompetence affects the performance of everyone in the school. Over time, even effective teachers might conclude, "Why bother?" and morale, as well as trust, may decrease, affecting all students. Even though taking on the role of monitor can diminish trust with the individuals in question, the *trust-building* leader understands her ethical responsibilities to the collective body of students.

When considering the incompetence of those you supervise, do not engage in trust-busting behaviors. Instead, take the advice offered by Robert Frost, "The best way out [of a problem] is through," and do the following:

1. KNOW EFFECTIVE TEACHING STRATEGIES. You have to know what incompetence looks like. For example, you have to know what good teaching is and is not. To improve your competence in this area, you can learn techniques in teacher evaluation and effective classroom practices. You can attend training with your teachers or facilitate book studies about teaching.

2. USE PERSONNEL-MANAGEMENT TECHNIQUES. After you identify competence, you have to know how to address incompetence. You have to know how to evaluate and document the specific behaviors. You need to have knowledge of the laws of your state and the policies of your district. To address concerns, a good leader does not jump to a conclusion and threaten to fire the teacher. Rather the leader patiently asks questions, listens, and observes. The leader honestly states the concerns and provides specific feedback. When there is a lack of progress, the process becomes more formal, following the practices of effective documentation and supervision.

3. BE PERSISTENT. After you can identify and address incompetence, you must be persistent in your efforts. Addressing incompetence will be time-consuming, but an effective leader will make this commitment a priority. People will learn by your persistence and follow-through. Their trust in you will grow because they understand how serious you are about competence.

For Further Reflection

1. Who are the individuals in your school who might lack competence in areas of their job performances? What evidence do you have, or what evidence might you gather?
2. What difficulties do you have when addressing problems with employees?
3. How does a teacher's incompetence affect the morale of your organization and others' trust in you?
4. How do your supervisors manage incompetent employees? Do your supervisors gain trust or lose trust through their management of incompetence?

Remember

Some leaders lack the skills or courage to address employees with performance concerns. As you consider the aspect of trust, consider your courage and skill in addressing incompetence.

"I Prefer Group Reprimands"

Don't be a fault finder, don't be reprimanding people all the time.
—BENJAMIN FRANKLIN

Have you worked for someone who gave group reprimands (jokingly, we sometimes call these group beatings)? Jim was such a leader. Jim, a principal in a large high school, had a strict policy about teachers reporting to work on time—7:45 A.M., which was about 15 minutes before the students' first class. When teachers arrived late, students entered empty classrooms. Jim believed that these situations caused many problems related to safety and that the teachers' tardiness gave a negative message to students about being prepared.

Still, teachers arrived late. And most of the time, it was the same three or four people. In the monthly faculty meetings, Jim would remind everyone to be on time. As the problem continued, he lectured the teachers in the meetings. Ironically, the teachers who were tardy did not listen, and sometimes they were not present at the meetings. However, the other 50 punctual teachers heard the message. Some of the teachers who sometimes arrived a few minutes before the deadline thought that maybe he was directing his message to them. So, the meeting ended on a negative note for 50 punctual teachers.

Although providing warnings and reprimands in a large group is not an automatic trust buster, the continued practice of addressing a group about the problems of a few can be. Jim needed to address the problem individually with those who were late. Providing group reprimands was frustrating for the other teachers because they witnessed an unresolved problem and a leader who continued to reprimand everyone for the misconduct of a few.

Can you remember a time that you were part of a group that received a reprimand for the actions of a few? If the leader continued with this strategy, how might you perceive her effectiveness? Many leaders take this approach of group reprimands, hoping that the bad behavior will be stopped immediately. Sometimes, a leader writes an e-mail to everyone, hoping this action will save time and remedy the issue quickly. Unfortunately, this strategy rarely succeeds—the targeted individuals often think the leader is talking about someone else, and the innocent teachers might think they have done something wrong. Others observe that the bad behaviors continue and sometimes conclude that the leader is ineffective.

So how do you address problems without reprimanding the whole group?

1. ADDRESS CONCERNS IN PRIVATE. You still address the problem, but not in a large group. Teachers should hear about performance concerns in a private meeting, face-to-face. In this way, the teachers understand your expectations and know that you mean what you say.

2. AVOID SHAME TACTICS. Never shame or embarrass people, especially in a group setting. Intentionally embarrassing someone breaks trust with him and with many of the observers who are empathizing with him. Leaders who shame others in group settings often experience difficulty building trust.

3. CLARIFY PROCEDURES AND EXPECTATIONS. When might you address a concern in a large group setting? You might bring up a situation if you think that teachers are not aware of the expectations or procedures. For example, you have invited several guest speakers to visit with your students during assemblies. Do the teachers know your expectations? Do you expect teachers to accompany their classes to the assembly? Do you expect the teachers to be attentive, or may they grade papers while they are listening? Should they check messages on their phones? Clarifying procedures and expectations can be acceptable in a large group if the focus is truly intended for informing and not reprimanding.

Try to keep the focus of large group meetings positive and about learning. Getting an entire faculty together on a regular basis can be challenging, so treat this time as a valuable resource. With the large group, spend time talking about the school's mission, applauding the efforts of individuals and teams, sharing what is working in the classrooms, and learning about topics that support students.

For Further Reflection

1. How do your supervisors address the mistakes or misconduct of your peers? Individually or in a group? Verbally or in writing?
2. How do your supervisors' actions in regard to addressing misconduct build or break the trust you have with them?
3. If you were making mistakes, how would you want your supervisors to address your actions?
4. Have you ever been embarrassed in a group setting by a supervisor? How did the situation affect your trust levels with the supervisor?
5. Leaders can build or break trust with how they handle the mistakes of others. To what extent do you agree or disagree with this statement?
6. How do you address the mistakes or misconduct of others? Individually or in a group? Verbally or in writing?

Remember

Even when it seems most expedient to address the misbehaviors of a few in a large group setting or in a group e-mail, reconsider. One can build trust by addressing concerns individually and using large group meetings for praise and learning.

"I Like Drama"

If there seems to be drama wherever you go,
consider the fact that you might be the one bringing it!

—ANONYMOUS

Effective leaders generally have a healthy sense of themselves. Sometimes we call this ego, and some studies have shown that the best leaders have strong egos. These leaders are confident and believe that they can make a difference. However, managing one's sense of self requires awareness. Leaders who allow their egos to run wild risk breaking trust with their followers for many reasons. The actions of these drama queens (and kings) are trust busters because they are unpredictable and create an emotionally unsafe work environment.

Think about someone for whom you have worked who demonstrated a need to be the center of attention much of the time. In many situations, such individuals insert themselves as the focus. Perhaps they have vital information to add to the problem or the perfect solution to save the day. They tend to monopolize conversations and meetings; rarely are they speechless. Regardless of the situation, drama queens and kings make a big deal out of lots of things.

Drama queens and kings often have high energy and are easily bored. They can generate problems when few exist. Some are known to "awful-ize" situations with predictions stated as facts. Even though one would think they have huge egos, they often tend to be very insecure. Frequently, they cover this insecurity by creating constant activity around them and sometimes even anxiety. They tend to be connected with many people and gather much of their information through speculation and gossip. They often insert themselves into others' business, without minding their own. They break trust with others because their behaviors and words are unpredictable. They create unstable environments based on their need to generate activity.

We have worked for both drama queens and kings—gender does not seem to be a factor. Cindy, an admitted drama queen, monopolized meetings with her staff and with her colleagues. She talked much of the time and offered opinions and hearsay about the problems at hand. When the economy worsened, Cindy speculated and discussed the worst-case scenarios of teachers losing their jobs. She spoke with such authority that many teachers believed she had inside information about the school board's future decisions. When the decisions were actually made, some positions were cut but no teachers lost their jobs, due to attrition. By this time, Cindy had moved on and created many more dramas.

What can leaders do if they realize they are engaging in trust-busting behavior because of their need for drama?

1. SELF-ASSESS. First, you can examine your own behaviors. In conversations or group meetings, do you tend to turn the conversation toward yourself? Do you tend to interrupt and insert your opinions frequently? Do you find that your day is often filled with "fighting fires"? Do others believe that you tend to make a bigger deal out of things than is needed? Being honest about your own attention needs will help you gain awareness about the harmful effects of these behaviors.

2. PRACTICE THE STOP STRATEGY. One strategy leaders can use when they realize they are susceptible to drama is the "stop" technique, similar to a time-out. People prone to drama sometimes experience a rush (or high) that follows a crisis. The rush can be related to the stress chemicals released during the fight-or-flight response. Over time, when leaders recognize this reaction, they can say, "Stop." They can visualize raising a hand in a stop position or verbalizing the word *stop* to themselves. Then, leaders can ask themselves, "Is this really a problem? What do we know for sure right now?" Stopping, even for a moment, as simple as it seems, can be a key in helping leaders change their reactions and become trust builders rather than trust busters.

For Further Reflection

1. Think about the drama queens and kings you have known. Are they trustworthy? Why or why not?
2. What do these drama queens and kings do that breaks trust with others?
3. To what extent do you enjoy being the center of attention or being the one who solves the problems at work?
4. To what extent do you make a big deal out of small things?

Remember

Creating unnecessary drama in the workplace is an action that breaks trust. Leaders can build trust by monitoring their responses and managing their need for attention.

"I Want You to Get Over It, Already!"

*My mama always said you've got to put the past behind you
before you can move on.*

—Forrest Gump

Leaders who convey the attitude of "get over it" can harm trust. When the leader tells teachers, parents, and students to just get over something, he is sending a message that he is not tuned in to others' needs, not sensitive to the larger issues, unwilling to listen, and not empathetic. This attitude shows that the leader does not care how others are feeling. Often, such leaders cannot understand how others are feeling about an experience or event when they insist that individuals need to move past whatever the issue is and just get over it.

Leaders are very busy. As leaders, after listening to a complaint, we typically consider that the issue is resolved. Perhaps we may think that the issue was not a big deal in the first place. Leaders with the mantra "just get over it" sometimes are proud of their quickness to action and consider this no-nonsense approach a sign of their strong leadership. They are often so proud of this approach to leadership that they are unaware that their actions are trust busters instead of trust builders. Leaders with the "just get over it" philosophy are likely lacking in qualities that build and boost trust, such as empathy, good listening, and concern for others.

You might be thinking, "My job is so busy, and I really don't have time for insignificant items." Although many leaders share this sentiment, sometimes the insignificant items people bring to you can become like little buzzing gnats—insignificant, it is true, but a huge bother. If the biggest complaints and problems that you frequently deal with are little things, you might take a moment to count your blessings. Instead of telling people to "just get over it," take a moment to listen and show your concern. Do not think that by brushing these individuals and their concerns aside that they will go away. No, they will simply reappear again and again until the problem is solved or until they are finally able to move on. Thus, little insignificant issues become major problems when there is a lack of trust.

What actions can you take to change the trust-busting behaviors that convey to others to "just get over it"? Consider the following example of a teacher who has lost a significant amount of budget money due to cuts in the district. As leader, you are aware that this shortfall has occurred throughout the district, not just at your school or in her classroom. You have shared this information with everyone. You have had at least one other discussion with this teacher regarding the loss of her budget money. The next time she sees you and begins her complaint, instead of responding with annoyance and the "just get over it" attitude, invite her to come into your office and ask her to restate her case. This time, try to listen in a different way. Try to understand her source of frustration, the other stresses in her life, and perhaps the other times she has felt slighted in the district. Often, there is more to the story than the issue itself.

Although empathetic listening will not restore the budget, it might allow this teacher to know that she has been heard and that you genuinely care. Possibly, when you are both engaged in this conversation, together you might discover creative ways to address this budget issue. Sometimes people cannot get over things because no one has listened to them to help them feel heard and understood. Sometimes they just need someone to genuinely experience their lives for a minute, to be in their shoes. By showing your concern, you enable the individual to get over the issue with grace and, more importantly, to move on to new challenges. When you change your trust-busting behavior from "just get over it" to that of a leader who genuinely cares about the issues and concerns of others, you become a trust builder.

For Further Reflection

1. Think back to the last time your actions conveyed "just get over it" to someone. You may have used these very words, or your voice may have sounded annoyed. How might you rebuild trust with that individual?

2. In what situations are you more likely to demonstrate the attitude of "just get over it"? What can you do to address this pattern?

3. With whom are you more likely to demonstrate the "just get over it" attitude? Why might this pattern exist?

4. What are some ways that you might develop a better relationship with staff members in a way that they will know you consider their concerns?

Remember

When a leader changes the trust-busting behavior of "just get over it" to one of listening and caring about the issues and concerns of others, the leader can build trust with others.

TRUST BUSTER

"Do What I Say, Not What I Do"

What you do speaks so loudly that I cannot hear what you say.

—Ralph Waldo Emerson

Have you ever driven with teenagers who were new drivers as passengers? If they are like most teens, they point out every rolling stop, every time you creep above the speed limit, and every yellow light that you rush through. They seem to notice every mistake you make. In fact, maybe insurance companies should have a special discount for drivers who have teenage passengers—it is like having a full-time defensive driving instructor ride with you each step of the way. As parents, we want our children to learn how to drive safely, but some days we aren't the best models. Our passengers might notice our bad driving habits, but we don't want them to copy these habits. This situation confirms the age-old adage that actions speak louder than words, whether it occurs in the car with children or at work with colleagues.

As a school leader, you must be ready to model the behavior you expect of others. When you tell teachers, parents, students, and others to behave a certain way but then choose not to engage in that type of behavior yourself, you send the message that your standards are different, that perhaps you think you're superior to them, or that a different set of rules applies to you.

Unfortunately, "do what I say, not what I do" does not build trust. Trust is about congruence and alignment. People are more likely to be trusted when their words match their actions. Intuitively, we trust people more when their nonverbal behaviors align with their words. Much trust is broken when your followers discover this lack of alignment.

For example, in a school, you might talk to your teachers about such issues as frequent tardiness or absences. Yet over time, the teachers observe that you arrive late or that you are absent often. Perhaps you emphasize the importance of treating parents and students in a respectful manner, yet you fail to treat teachers with respect. Hypocritical behavior is a huge trust buster. Too often, leaders do not reflect upon their own behaviors and continue to act inconsistently.

If you say you want people to work hard, but you put forth minimal effort, then it is difficult to build trust. You cannot make it difficult for teachers who have doctor's appointments and then leave early yourself because your schedule is more flexible. One of the biggest differences is the way your time is structured and used. Teachers are captive in their classrooms. They cannot leave and do not have the flexibility to check out early. When they are absent, learning at school must continue. Sometimes, your schedule is the same way. You cannot be absent and you cannot be late, even though you have more flexibility than teachers do. Do not abuse the power that your position has to offer.

As the leader, you are on stage. All eyes are on you. You do not have to be perfect; in fact, it's more endearing when you are not, but people want a leader who is worthy of trust and respect. Leaders concerned about trust know that they must watch for duplicity and congruence. These leaders who want to build trust hold themselves to the same standards, or even higher standards, than they expect others to meet. They surround themselves with individuals who give them information about incongruent behaviors.

For Further Reflection

1. How do I handle issues of absences and doctors' appointments? Do I handle these issues differently for different people? How do I handle them for myself?

2. Why is it important for me to do the jobs I ask others to do?

3. Think of a recent example when your actions were not congruent with your words. What can you do differently next time?

4. Who would be able to tell you examples of behaviors that do not match your actions? (For more information on assessing trust levels, see Trust Booster #1: Assess Trust.)

Remember

Behave in such a way that if your colleagues modeled your actions, they would be ideal employees. Remember that a "do what I say, not what I do" approach makes you seem like a hypocrite and can be a real trust buster.

"Inconsiderate and Insensitive? Who, Me?"

Knowledge has never been known to enter the head through an open mouth.

—Doug Larson

One of the most common ways that leaders bust trust is acting in ways that are insensitive or inconsiderate of others. The leaders we know who were perceived in this way were not bad people. Sometimes they were likeable. In fact, we believe that they could not see that their behaviors were insensitive, inconsiderate, or offensive. Some of the common behaviors in which insensitive, inconsiderate leaders engage are telling inappropriate jokes, making comments that hurt feelings, being sarcastic, and stereotyping people. All of these behaviors, when practiced on a regular basis, can harm the development of trust with everyone.

One principal in particular began every faculty meeting by telling a joke. She shared jokes that made fun of women with blonde hair, people who were overweight, the elderly, coaches, secretaries, teenagers, parents, and people of different ethnic groups. Faculty members would pause before they entered the meeting room and take a deep breath, wondering who might be offended during the meeting. Whenever teachers saw the principal talking and laughing with someone, they automatically assumed that someone was the butt of a joke.

Many years ago, another leader constantly referred to his office staff as "the girls" and his women faculty as "my own harem." Many people believed that these comments were inconsiderate and offensive. Today, these comments could be considered sexual harassment. Another year, one of the teachers had a newborn, and she returned to work when the baby was a few weeks old. The assistant principal suggested that for a few weeks, the teacher be assigned to an afternoon schedule rather than a morning schedule as a way to help her. Instead of accepting this suggestion, the principal remarked that changes could not be made for everyone with a need, and assigned her morning duty. The principal missed an opportunity to show consideration and build trust with the teacher.

So how do you overcome trust-buster behavior that is viewed as insensitive, inconsiderate, or just plain offensive? Following these few ideas will help build trust at your school:

1. THINK *BEFORE* YOU SPEAK. Sometimes when you think before you speak, you will decide it is best not to speak at all. As Albert Einstein noted, "If A equals success, then the formula is A = X + Y + Z. X is work. Y is play. Z is keep your mouth shut." When you think about your intentions and your word choice before you speak, you can sometimes avoid trust-busting language.

2. THINK *WHILE* YOU SPEAK. Listen to what you are saying when you are talking. Gauge the reaction of the individual to whom you are speaking. This can be a helpful guide to make sure that your speech does not offend others.

3. THINK *AFTER* YOU SPEAK. Develop the habit of reflecting on what you have said. Did it sound right? Was it appropriate? Could it have been stated in a better way? If you decide what you said appeared insensitive, inconsiderate, or offensive, go to the individual immediately and say you are sorry.

Leaders must remember that humor does have a place in schools, but it must be appropriate and never at the expense of another person or groups of people. A joke I have often shared is about a time I was eating at a fancy restaurant. I was wearing a shawl. Without noticing, I picked up the end of the shawl, instead of my napkin, and dabbed daintily at my mouth. When I realized what I had done, I burst out laughing and others who had observed this laughed with me. Everyone laughs now when I share this story. This type of humor is okay; I can make fun of myself. I just should not make fun of others.

Get to know the personal circumstances of those with whom you work, and do what you can to make the place of work one that is sensitive and considerate of others. There are times when you will want to consider special situations. Examples could be adjusting schedules for employees caring for aging parents or attending to other family matters.

For Further Reflection

1. Think about something that you said recently that might have been inappropriate. Do you think anyone was offended? If so, go to that individual and make amends. If your inappropriate comment was made in a group setting, let the group know that you were wrong.

2. Download jokes from the Internet so that you have a ready cache of appropriate jokes to bring humor to a meeting. Here is one website: www.ahajokes.com.

3. Think about the personal circumstances of your faculty and students. Identify those who need to be treated with extra sensitivity right now.

Remember

Leaders build trust by being sensitive and considerate of the feelings of others. Trust-building leaders avoid laughing at or telling inappropriate jokes, making comments that hurt feelings, being sarcastic, and stereotyping people.

"It's Not My Fault"

To find fault is easy; to do better may be difficult.

—PLUTARCH

We all know the basics of dodgeball—kids throw the ball at a group of opponents. You try to not get hit by moving around. If the ball touches you, you are out and have to stand and watch everyone else continue playing. The person throwing the ball tries to get everyone out so she wins. Having an "it's not my fault" attitude is like a game of dodgeball. Someone keeps throwing the ball, trying to get everyone else out, while others keep dodging the objects thrown their way. Playing dodgeball in work situations is one way leaders break trust.

Do you know someone with an "it's not my fault" type of attitude? Regardless of what happens, he always has a good reason why the problem belongs to someone else. For example, we recently had a faculty meeting where we discussed declining standardized test scores. The purpose of the meeting was to develop strategies for improving our curriculum and instruction so that scores would also improve. Immediately, one of our team members began discussing how some students were not good test takers and that the test was not indicative of what students needed to know. These two statements may be true (or not), but the purpose of the meeting was not to place blame or to identify problems with the tests. Instead, the purpose was to focus on improvement. Nevertheless, this person continued to focus on whose fault it was that scores were low, and the fault never seemed to be ours as the group of educators. The problem with this approach, at its most basic level, is that if it is always somebody else's fault, then how are we empowered to make things better?

Do you know individuals who rarely think things are their fault? Maybe they are very competent and capable people who do not make many mistakes. However, when something happens involving them, they find a way to point out "it's not my fault." They may not necessarily use those words in order to lay blame on someone else. Maybe they immediately blow up and divert the attention elsewhere. Maybe they argue, get defensive, storm out of a meeting, or make excuses. Maybe they immediately find other people or circumstances to blame. These are actually common responses, and accepting responsibility for something that does not turn out as planned can be tough. However, "it's not my fault" prevents any positive change in direction from taking place.

When individuals cannot stop and be honest about a situation, when they cannot fairly evaluate the situation and their role in it, when they cannot accept some ownership of the problem, solving problems becomes very difficult, if not impossible, and relationships are strained. We often develop trust by showing the whole of who we are, including our more vulnerable sides. When we do not acknowledge our part in a large process and instead spend our efforts avoiding the blame and putting the blame on others, we delay the solution and we forgo the chance to show that we are human. All of us, no matter how competent or intelligent we may be, make mistakes and contribute to problems. The key to not damaging trust in these situations is the willingness to address mistakes or problems, including our role in them, and move forward.

Some experts recommend that the leader should assume a large part of the responsibility when things go wrong. Why? Several reasons make this a good approach for leaders. First, accepting responsibility allows everyone to put the blame game aside and move on to problem solving. Assigning blame rarely matters; when it does matter, you can deal with that issue separately and privately with the responsible party. Second, removing blame from a situation allows everyone, yourself included, to focus and remain focused on solutions. Finally, accepting the responsibility shows teachers that the staff is a team and will stand together in both good and bad situations. When your school has failures or problems, as every school will, step up, accept responsibility, and lead your group to find a better way. Do not waste energy on dodging the blame. Step out of that game and do as Henry Ford said: "Don't find fault. Find a remedy."

An additional strategy for accepting responsibility and avoiding the blame game is to reflect on your motivation. If you sometimes find yourself saying, "It's not my fault," think about why that may be. What might you be afraid of—that you will look incompetent? That you might be wrong? That someone is going to berate you or embarrass you? That you mustn't ever make mistakes or be wrong? A deeper, reflective look at why you try to assign blame or avoid responsibility is helpful in many ways. Insecurities, fears, or patterns of behaviors from the past could be contributing to your actions. A personal analysis of these motivations can help you understand these behaviors and develop a more positive, effective approach to handling difficult situations.

For Further Reflection

1. Think about the system in which you work. How are mistakes handled? What are some of the cultural rules about making mistakes where you work?

2. What types of mistakes do you think are acceptable to make? What types do you find inexcusable? How do you handle it when others make mistakes?

3. What might be a situation in which people tend to focus on who is to blame or who is at fault? What strategies can you use to help avoid these types of attitudes and to refocus people on a more positive approach to resolving the situation?

4. Why does having an "it's not my fault" attitude break trust? How does it impact others? How does this attitude make it difficult to develop trust?

Remember

Learning to accept being wrong or making a mistake is an important step in building trust. Accepting responsibility gives you the chance to show that you are human and that you can accept and learn from mistakes, even when they are not your own.

"Leave Me Alone"

*I never said, "I want to be alone." I only said,
"I want to be left alone." There is all the difference.*

—GRETA GARBO

O ne of the most powerful ways for leaders to break trust with others is really quite simple—being unavailable. Leaders who are not accessible to others use several trust-busting actions to assure that they are left alone. For example, they manage to appear busy most of the time. This strategy works very well because most people will not "bother" you if they feel that you are busy or too involved in something else. When you do find inaccessible leaders in their offices, their administrative assistants usually have been given strict instructions to allow no one in without making an appointment—all under the guise of protecting the leaders' valuable time.

Leaders who want to be left alone are especially effective at being difficult to find. Instead of being available to help, to answer questions, or to talk with others, these leaders are not at school, or if they are at school, no one knows where they are. These trust-busting leaders are rarely seen in the halls, in the cafeteria, or on the playground. When the bell rings and the buses are loading, they conveniently disappear and are not around to supervise or offer assistance.

Another common action specific to maintaining this "leave me alone" attitude is the hand. When inaccessible leaders are approached by a teacher, a parent, or even a student, the hand often goes up, followed by the words, "Not now; this is not an appropriate place for this conversation. Check with my secretary to find an available time." In this case, the leaders are counting on the teacher, parent, or student not to follow up with the needed conversation.

Leaders who are not accessible tend to send a message to others that suggests that the needs of others are trivial. Consequently, constituents do not feel listened to, which often means that issues at the school go unaddressed.

So what actions can you take to change the trust-busting behavior of being inaccessible? Here are three suggestions:

1. Schedule a time every day to be in high-need areas: the hallways, parking lots, and the cafeteria.
2. With your secretaries, review office policies for scheduling meetings and handling unannounced visitors.
3. Establish an open-door policy with guidelines so that staff members feel welcome to stop by and have a general idea of when you are available (such as before school, during lunch, and/or after school).

School leaders do need uninterrupted times to accomplish required tasks. The key is to communicate and be transparent with your coworkers. Some leaders block off a specific time each day or week to accomplish reports and paperwork. Others stay late or come in early to find quiet times to concentrate without distractions. There will be times that you need to shut your office door or find a quiet place to work to accomplish tasks that require attention to detail. However, leaders concerned about building trust know that they have to balance all of their tasks and find times to be available to others.

For Further Reflection

1. Think back to yesterday. How available were you to teachers, parents, and students?
2. What does your body language say when others approach

you? Are you inviting? Are you silently saying, "I want to be left alone"?

3. If you find yourself wanting to be left alone too often, consider why.

4. How do you balance the tasks that require concentration with the need to be present and available?

Remember

One of the most visible ways leaders convey the attitude they want to be left alone is simply to not be accessible.

"I Expect Perfection"

If you look for perfection, you'll never be content.
—LEO TOLSTOY

As leaders, we set high standards and expect people to perform at their best. However, there can be a fine line between having high expectations and being a perfectionist. When we have high standards, this desire can mean that we want the best for our schools, our faculty, our students, and ourselves. We want people to work hard and reap the rewards of this hard work. But hard work rarely, if ever, results in perfection. In fact, perfection is unattainable, both at the individual and organizational levels. Because perfection is not a realistic goal, setting standards of perfection can be a real trust buster.

How is being a perfectionist a trust buster? Unlike high standards, which encourage people to perform at their best and reward hard work, perfection focuses on what is not right and what is missing. Being a perfectionist sends the message that someone's work is not good enough. Perfectionists frequently have additional ideas and more suggestions to change a finished project. The problem is that when your standards are too high, people cannot meet them and become frustrated. Ultimately, people become discouraged because what they do is never enough, and too often, they give up trying.

Working for a perfectionist is a real challenge. Sometimes, regardless of how nice the person is, a perfectionist can be the most dreaded of bosses. Faculty members may feel enormous stress trying to meet the standards of their perfectionist boss. Trying to please a perfectionist can mean working long hours, beyond what might normally be expected. It also means having your work scrutinized on a regular basis. What the perfectionist may perceive to be constructive feedback comes across as constant criticism of others' work. For many of us, that type of criticism can be hard to take on a regular basis.

Evaluate your own style of work. Do you see perfectionist tendencies? Sometimes these tendencies are very difficult to see in ourselves. To help recognize perfectionist behaviors that could make working for you difficult and that could jeopardize trust among you and your colleagues, ask yourself the following questions:

- Do you think you are the only one who can do something, or at least the only one who can do it right?
- Do you think your ideas are the best or that there is only one way to do things?
- Do others say you micromanage?
- Do you correct everyone's work?
- Do you require that everything go through you first?
- Do you point out errors in front of others?
- Are you overly concerned about what others will think of your work?
- Do you find that you are rarely or ever satisfied with the work of others? Or your own work?

If you answered yes to three or more of the questions, then you may need to consider carefully the impression you are making with coworkers. You might be sending a message that you require perfection and that others do not have what it takes to measure up to your expectations. Be purposeful in your interactions with others when they are working on tasks that you have assigned or delegated. Decide what is acceptable and what is not, and communicate these expectations clearly.

Now, continue your self-assessment with a few more questions:

- Are you generous with praise?
- Do you understand the difference between "good enough" and "perfect"?
- Are you realistic about projects and the time they will take to complete?
- Do you delegate tasks to others, including important tasks?
- Do you recognize the strengths in others and ask for help?

If the answer to several of these questions is yes, then you have a good understanding of the difference between high expectations and perfection. Praising others and setting clear boundaries about what quality of work is acceptable can be very positive steps toward building trust with others. Delegating important tasks lets people know that you trust them to do a good job and that you recognize they have important contributions to make to the school or district. These questions can help you keep your standards of perfection in check and serve as a reminder of strategies available to support others who work with you.

Part of what makes a perfectionist so critical of others' work is a fear of being judged by others. In reality, perfectionists are constantly judging themselves. The behaviors that perfectionists criticize or correct in others are often the very actions that they find in themselves as well. Do you believe that mistakes are unacceptable, including your own? Do you feel you must prove yourself to others? Do you suffer anxiety about projects until they are complete? Do you work harder than anyone around you? Do you forget to focus on the progress made and instead focus on the mistakes? If so, these perfectionist qualities may be affecting the trust you are able to build and maintain at work.

One way to compensate for these behaviors is to acknowledge and admit that you are a perfectionist. People are much more forgiving of the flaws that we readily own. You can also laugh about your issues with perfection; having a sense of humor is helpful. Make a conscious effort to offer praise to others (authentic praise, of course) and to keep criticism to a minimum. Decide in advance at what level a project must be completed and the amount of time that should be given to the project, and then hold yourself to those limits. Ask for feedback from others about your behavior. Focus on priorities: decide what is most important and learn to differentiate; not everything is important.

Also ban yourself from the idea that if you want something done right, you have to do it yourself. Instead, address others' poor work quality directly and individually as appropriate. And at the same time, remind yourself that mistakes are normal and to be expected. Salvador Dalí summed up perfection with the following quote: "Have no fear of perfection—you'll never reach it."

For Further Reflection

1. Do you have perfectionist tendencies?
2. Do you work with someone who expects perfection? If so, how does her perfectionism affect your relationship?
3. How do you differentiate between high standards and perfection?

> ### Remember
> As leaders, we set high standards and expect people to perform at their best. However, expecting perfection from others or from ourselves is unrealistic and can damage our ability to build trust.

#11

"I'm in Love with My Ideas"

If you have an apple and I have an apple and we exchange these apples then you and I will still each have one apple. But if you have an idea and I have an idea and we exchange these ideas, then each of us will have two ideas.

—GEORGE BERNARD SHAW

Being a leader with big ideas can be a great trust builder. However, if you are not careful, it can just as easily cause you to be a trust buster. An important element of trust is how leaders handle the daily solving of problems in the organization or school. There are many situations that need solutions, and there is never a shortage of problems that demand to be addressed. This is why it is so important for leaders to be people with big ideas; however, some individuals with big ideas frequently break trust in how they handle the generation of ideas and the implementation of possible solutions.

Trust busters who are in love with their ideas have no shortage of ideas and no shortage of willingness to share their ideas. In fact, they are often so busy creating good ideas to solve problems in their schools, they do not even see that they are actually creating more problems than they are solving.

Consider the principal of a middle school where teachers reported increasing problems with student behavior during lunchtime. Some issues were students throwing food, being rude to the cafeteria workers, and fighting. Lunchtime misbehavior was escalating, and a solution was needed. After reflecting, the principal decided to assign additional teachers to lunch duty. Informally, the principal discussed the problem and her solution with several staff members and administrators. Some asked questions, trying to understand the problem better. Some volunteered other ideas that would contribute to the solution. But the principal was so in love with her own idea that she dismissed these questions and solutions. Instead, she e-mailed all the teachers with changes to the duty schedule that would begin immediately. As might be expected, there was much discussion among the teachers about this quick "solution" to the problem. Some teachers did not read the e-mail, some showed up late for their new duty, some reviewed state policies about duty schedule changes, and some thought about contacting school board members. Now, the principal had an even bigger problem than student misbehavior at lunch—she had a trust problem with her staff. Her unwillingness to consider others' solutions became a trust buster.

Being in love with one of your ideas despite the suggestions, cautions, and advice of others will not automatically result in lowering trust. However, when a leader is characterized as pushing his ideas through even when others express concerns, his actions can harm relationships. Leaders who are so in love with their ideas that they cannot listen to the ideas (and concerns) of others create problems that lead to long-term trust issues.

What actions can you take to change the trust-busting behaviors that convey to others you are in love with *your* ideas? Recognize that no matter how much you know about an issue, you cannot have all the information needed all the time. In the case of the principal with the lunchroom misbehavior, she failed to recognize the impact that changing a schedule would have, and she failed to study the problem to understand the multiple causes and contributors to the problem. Trust busters who are in love with their own ideas do not understand that there is rarely one best answer. Thus, there is wisdom in listening to others, and this principal failed to systemically consider options and then generate support for a proposed solution.

Decisions impacting a number of staff have far-reaching consequences in issues of trust, morale, and long-term success. Instead of
being a trust buster who is in love with your own ideas, try doing the
following:

- Be sure that suggested changes are based on data and are truly
  necessary.
- Be able to explain the circumstances clearly so that everyone
  can understand the problems that need resolution.
- Tell people your ideas and listen to their ideas; when possible,
  incorporate their ideas into the solution.

When you change the trust-busting behavior "I'm in love with *my*
ideas" to that of a leader who has creative ideas but involves other
stakeholders (educators, parents, and students) in listening to and
refining those ideas, you become a trust builder. And, you will likely
have better ideas to implement.

For Further Reflection

1. To what extent are you receptive to the suggestions of others
   after you have presented your ideas?
2. To what extent do you believe in the possibility of multiple
   appropriate solutions?
3. How does the need to find quick solutions affect the quality of
   decisions that are made in your organization?

Remember

A trust-building leader is one who has creative ideas but
involves other stakeholders (educators, parents, and
students) in listening to and refining those ideas.

"I Take Things Personally"

We often add to our pain and suffering by being overly sensitive,
over-reacting to minor things and sometimes taking things
too personally.

—14TH DALAI LAMA

Being a school leader is a complicated job. The average principal works many hours a week handling stress-related issues regarding personnel, students, parents, instruction, budgets, and a myriad of other topics. Because the job of a school leader is so challenging, administrators, dealing with fatigue and exhaustion, can be sensitive and take things too personally. Taking things personally is more likely to happen when leaders are under constant pressure and do not take time to recuperate and gain the fresh perspective that breaks allow. Regardless of the reason for taking things too personally, this action is a trust buster.

Consider a teacher who approaches a principal after school and casually remarks about the chaos in the lunchroom. Typically, a leader might engage in further conversation about the lunchroom problem and brainstorm solutions. Perhaps a leader would respond with humor about a full moon. Some leaders might take the comment personally and respond defensively: "I can't be everywhere!" When leaders conclude that comments and criticisms are about their personal failings, the trust levels with teachers can plummet.

So, what can you do to stop taking things personally and begin to build trust with others? Here are some suggestions:

1. TAKE A DEEP BREATH. Give people the benefit of the doubt. Do not assume that comments, such as the example mentioned previously, are intended to be critical of you. The teacher in the example might have made an observation without intending to attribute the problem to the principal's absence.

2. DON'T MAKE IT ABOUT YOU. Do not conclude that negative statements about events that happened at school are directed at you. Even if you have trouble convincing yourself, act as if they are not about you so that you can focus on solutions.

3. STEP BACK. Develop emotional detachment. Emotional detachment does not mean that you do not care or that you have no emotions about something; it simply means that you assertively work at maintaining a certain distance or lack of emotionality when faced with the demands of others.

4. BE STRATEGIC. Recognize which individuals tend to rub you the wrong way. Awareness of who these people are will help you better monitor your responses.

Leaders who want to work on not taking things personally should become familiar with or review the concepts of emotional intelligence. Emotional intelligence describes one's capacity to "perceive emotions, assimilate emotion-related feelings, understand the meaning of the emotions, and manage them" (Mayer, Caruso, & Salovey, 1999, p. 267). Additional resources that might be helpful to leaders can be located at www.unh.edu/emotional_intelligence/index.html. As leaders improve their self-awareness skills related to emotions, they can improve in the management of the emotions. By understanding how to manage emotions, leaders will be more likely not to take things personally.

For Further Reflection

1. Reflect on the most recent times when you have responded too sensitively or too personally to professional issues. Can you detect any patterns? Is the tendency to take things personally happening during specific periods of the day? Or does it happen more often with certain individuals or around certain topics?

2. How self-aware are you? Consider how this self-awareness influences your decisions.

3. How well do you manage your emotions? Invite trusted peers to talk with you about how they perceive that you manage your emotions.

4. What strategies have you implemented when you believe that you are becoming emotional? Do you count to ten? Do you admit you are tired or stressed and defer the discussion for later? What other strategies might you use?

Remember

Because the job of the school leader is so difficult, one can become sensitive and take things personally. Regardless of the reason, taking things personally can turn into a trust buster.

"I've Changed My Mind Again"

All change is not growth, as all movement is not forward.
—ELLEN GLASGOW

Generally, the notion of being able to change one's mind is a positive attribute of leadership. After all, changing one's mind allows one to adapt to new experiences and to implement new ideas and new strategies. Consider the saying, "If nothing ever changed, there'd be no butterflies." Certainly no one wants a world without butterflies. However, when building trust in a school, a leader must be cautious about changing her mind too often. Unfortunately, too many leaders engage in the trust-busting behavior of changing their decisions constantly, seemingly capriciously.

Changing one's decisions too often causes teachers to conclude that their leader is inconsistent and indecisive. When Woodrow Wilson said, "If you want to make enemies, try to change something," he was not referring to the leader who changes his mind again and again. Most educators understand the importance of being flexible and open-minded. Instead, I would change Wilson's quote this way: "If you want to make enemies, try to change something . . . again and again." Too often, leaders can be indecisive and inconsistent such that teachers can no longer trust what they say. How many times have you heard someone say about a leader, "This may be his decision for now, but just wait until he talks to the next person. He will change his mind, you'll see."

A leader who changes his mind again and again is perceived as indecisive and inconsistent. This behavior is a trust buster because teachers and other staff members remain confused and uncertain. If the teachers act on a decision immediately and then the leader changes his mind, that situation becomes a problem. Yet, if the teachers take no action because they suspect a decision will be changed, that can be a problem. How long should they wait to implement the original decision? How can teachers trust a leader who changes his decisions too often? One teacher described working for her principal like "working for a yo-yo."

How can you change the trust-busting behavior of being wishy-washy into trust-building behaviors? Here are some ideas:

1. Do not make decisions too quickly.
2. Gather all the information needed from a variety of sources prior to making a decision.
3. If you do change your mind and make a different decision, communicate this change and your reasons with all who need to know.
4. Develop a network of trusted advisers, such as other leaders and staff members, who can provide wise counsel when you have to make a quick decision.
5. When you know you have already made a good decision, do not be influenced after the fact.

To build trust, faculty and staff need to have confidence in how you make decisions. They need to understand that when you change your mind it is because you have new and more complete information. They need to know that you are not changing your mind for capricious reasons.

For Further Reflection

1. Consider a decision that you made and then changed. Why did this change happen? What actions could you have taken to prevent being seen as inconsistent or indecisive?
2. Consider a decision that you made and then changed after someone influenced you. How did this change happen?
3. Create a list of trusted colleagues that you can contact when you need wise counsel.

Remember

Changing one's mind allows one to be adaptable, flexible, and open-minded and can contribute to building trust. However, leaders who change their minds frequently are viewed as indecisive and inconsistent, which is damaging to trust.

"I'm in a Bad Mood"

In thy face I see thy fury: if I longer stay
We shall begin our ancient bickerings.

—WILLIAM SHAKESPEARE

The face is not just a set of features; it is rather something that gives others a glimpse into our emotions. Our faces generally express the state of our emotions whether we are conscious of this or not. Consequently, our countenances offer others clues to predict our moods. Leaders who walk around the school with a frown or an angry expression are viewed as being in perpetually bad moods and are trust busters. A grumpy look seems to scream, "Don't bother me; something is wrong," and the message it sends is loud and clear.

Walking around the school with a worried, furrowed brow also conveys a bad mood. You may not be angry, but perhaps you are seriously concerned about something. This worried mood is communicated to others and, before you know it, faculty and staff are whispering about possible causes for the seriousness of your expression. Are their jobs at risk? What bad thing has happened or is going to happen? Because your expression seems so preoccupied with worry, others become worried. This action is a trust buster because, among other things, it sends the message that you, as the leader, obviously do not trust others enough to share your worry or concern with them.

Perhaps you are not grumpy, angry, or worried. Rather, you are unaware that your countenance is negative. Perhaps you do not realize that your face is making a statement about your mood to others that causes you to be perceived as moody, grumpy, angry, or worried, and thus unapproachable and untrusting. You can't walk around with a fake smile plastered on your face either. In fact, there is evidence that individuals can often tell if a smile is forced or genuine (Allen, Peterson, & Rhodes, 2006).

So how do you develop a countenance that does not announce a bad mood to others and change trust-busting actions to ones that build trust?

1. Be aware of your facial expressions. You might even glance in the mirror or review some photos that others have taken of you.
2. Spend time each day counting your blessings. This action will help you to think more positive thoughts throughout the day.
3. Some suggest that we should "act as if" when we are not feeling positive. This strategy is something that you can try, and with practice, you might be able to change a bad mood to one that is more positive. Writer Charles de Lint said, "The thing with pretending you're in a good mood is that sometimes you can."

If you have a genuine worry, find someone with whom you can share in confidence. Many times, the act of sharing a concern can reduce the level of anxiety. School leaders need a support system to help them manage the many challenging situations encountered in the job.

For Further Reflection

1. Are you communicating anger, annoyance, or worry when you do not intend to? Talk with a trusted friend about your countenance and the effect it might be having on others.
2. Do you see the glass as half empty or half full? What can you do to discipline yourself to think more positively rather than negatively?

3. When was a time that you effectively masked your emotions? How did this affect others? How did it affect you?

4. Do you have a genuine worry that can be shared with someone? Identify individuals, whether family or friends, who can assume this role of confidant.

5. Conduct an Internet search to learn more about the "act as if" technique. How can this technique be helpful when you are focused on changing habits that damage trust?

Remember

Trust-building leaders are aware of their body language and facial expressions. Leaders who walk around with sad, angry, or worried expressions can be trust busters.

TRUST BUSTER

"I Like to Gossip"

Whoever gossips to you will gossip about you.

—SPANISH PROVERB

Most people like to gossip sometimes, right? And if you listen to but do not repeat a story, then you're not really gossiping, right? And if nobody else knows about your actions or if the story is true, then there is no harm done, right? Wrong. Talking about colleagues, students, or others associated with work can be a major trust buster; in fact, gossip can be more like a trust destroyer. What may seem to be innocent conversation, regardless of your intent, can be very damaging to your work relationships.

Gossip comes in many forms. One resource defines gossip as "idle talk or rumor, especially about the personal or private affairs of others" (www.dictionary.com). The *Collins English Dictionary* defines gossip as "casual and idle chat; a conversation involving malicious chatter or rumours about other people." Perhaps you are talking about a person's marriage, her finances, or how she appeared in the grocery store. Perhaps the information is something someone told you directly, maybe even something he asked you not to tell. Or it might be something that you heard from someone else, where you were part of conversation that has been passed along. It might seem like innocent talk or interesting conversation. But if it does not serve a meaningful purpose for the business of the school, then your innocent conversation is actually gossip and it will likely be hurtful, both to you and to the person about whom you are talking.

As the school leader, the conversations you engage in are held to an even higher standard. It is important to remember that the teachers are professionals, your colleagues, your coworkers, and your partners in many ways, but they are not your friends when it comes to workplace conversations. Conversations with teachers and other staff can and should be warm, engaging, and friendly, but you, as the leader, must guard carefully against letting those conversations include unnecessary gossip. To paraphrase the police, anything you say can and will be used against you.

Gossip is a trust buster for many reasons. Talking about other people sends the message that you are not a safe person to talk to and that you can't be trusted, even if what you say is true and is never repeated beyond the listener. Participating in gossip communicates to people that you are willing to sacrifice, or at least risk, someone else's feelings or well-being for the sake of a good story or a laugh. If people cannot trust you to stay quiet when you hear something interesting or when they tell you something in confidence, then when can they trust you? The relationships that are hurt by idle talk can damage your effectiveness as a leader. And once words are uttered, they can't be taken back. Likewise, once the trust at your school has been damaged by gossip, it is very difficult to rebuild any level of integrity and respect among your teachers.

Before repeating anything you hear, ask yourself these questions: Are these words (a) kind? (b) true? and (c) necessary? If the answer to any of those questions is no, then you should definitely consider whether the comments need to be made in the first place. What positive outcome will result from the things you say?

For Further Reflection

1. Can you think of a time when you have had conversations about people or things at work that were not work-related? What was the purpose of that conversation? What results did it produce?

2. Have you been on the receiving end of workplace gossip? What were some of the harmful effects of that gossip?

3. What strategies can you develop to discourage unproductive talk in the workplace?

Remember

Gossip is harmful, no matter how interesting or innocent the comments may seem to be. Avoid conversations at work that are not productive.

TOOL 1: ASSESSMENT FOR TRUST BUSTERS			
Consider your actions as a leader. For each trust buster listed, ask yourself how often you are likely to exhibit that trust-busting behavior. Assessing your trust-busting behaviors can be a valuable experience.	RARELY	SOMETIMES	MOST OF THE TIME
1. I give opportunities for others to make suggestions, but I do not implement those ideas.			
2. I lack the skills or courage to address employees with performance concerns.			
3. I address the group about problems even when they involve only a few people who need correction.			
4. I find myself as the center of attention.			
5. I am impatient with individuals who are reluctant to move forward.			
6. My actions are not consistent with my words.			
7. I make comments that hurt others' feelings.			
8. When a mistake happens, I become defensive and focus on who is to blame.			
9. I let other administrators or secretaries handle a majority of the problems and concerns.			
10. I find that I am not satisfied with my work or others' work.			
11. I believe that my ideas for problem solving are better than most people's.			
12. I think that complaints and problems are my fault.			
13. I change my mind a lot before making a final decision.			
14. Others ask me, "What's wrong?" or say that I look like I am in a bad mood.			
15. I share confidential information with others.			

Evaluation

Congratulations! You had the courage to assess potential trust-busting behaviors. For areas that you marked "sometimes" or "most of the time," review the corresponding chapters for strategies that you can implement to change those trust-busting behaviors into trust-building behaviors. Consider what you can do to develop and improve on implementing these strategies. Be intentional in implementing strategies to help you build and boost trust.

PART II

Trust Builders

The ability to model and maintain trusting relationships is a critical leadership skill. High trust provides the platform for change and innovation. The following twenty-five trust builders describe many strategies that leaders can implement to build trust with the individuals in their school communities.

Understand Trust

Trust is like air; we don't notice it until it is polluted.

—ANONYMOUS

Trust, like air, is a complex balance of critical elements. You have likely worked in schools with excellent air quality and others with very polluted environments. By understanding the components of trust, leaders can be aware of how their actions affect the building's air quality.

Principals are often faced with difficult situations and challenges to change the instructional programs and outcomes of the school. Several researchers are discovering the important link between school improvement and trust (for more info, see Bryk & Schneider, 2002; Tschannen-Moran, 2004) and affirming that successful schools thrive in an environment of strong trust connections among teachers, parents, students, and leaders. Trust supports the difficult work of school improvement, but can easily be destroyed by the leader's behaviors.

Because leaders must enact change in today's schools, the development of trust can be tenuous. Even when leaders are well-intentioned, trust might not develop. Even when leaders are nice and caring people, trust might not develop. What, then, are the essentials of trust?

After reviewing many writings about trust, we envision trust as a combination of four qualities. The four Cs of trust are competence, care, character, and communication. Just as oxygen and nitrogen combine to form air, these qualities blend to form personal trustworthiness.

Competence

Have you ever had a bad haircut? Have you ever been to a dentist who had questionable practices? Did you return? As consumers, we expect those we trust with our hair or our teeth to have the knowledge and skills to do a good job. As with the services we receive, in our professional lives, trust and competence unite. What does competent leadership in education look like? It probably depends on whom you ask. Although the list of expectations is lengthy, a principal must be competent to create high-trust relationships with teachers. Teachers have further defined principal competence as the principal's ability to maintain a safe and orderly school, acquire needed resources, and appropriately respond to student behavior issues (Bryk & Schneider, 2002).

Care and Character

In past training sessions, when we have asked educators to describe trust, many list acts of kindness, care for others, and specific traits like integrity and reliability. Caring for others can include appreciation, gift giving, attention, and acts of service. In addition, leaders who use active listening and shared decision making show a regard for others. However, having concern for others is not enough; character is needed, too. Telling the truth, being transparent, and having courage are traits of trustworthy leaders. Finally, we cannot fake concern or character to manufacture trust; such duplicity reinforces distrust.

Communication

Studies show that employees have a higher level of satisfaction in organizations that communicate frequently regarding policies, decisions, and goals as opposed to those that provide limited information (Hamilton, 2001). On another level, words and tone reveal one's true intentions and feelings. Do your words model integrity and honesty? What are the assumptions behind your words? How do you handle frustration? How often do you criticize or belittle others? How do you handle those who openly disagree with you? Do you silence them with your authority, or do you truly seek to understand?

Understanding and Recognizing Trust Levels

Leaders who are trust builders know the importance of understanding and recognizing the trust levels in the school or within the district. Low trust levels, like polluted air, are difficult to detect. Often, leaders are unaware of the trust pollution until everyone is gasping for air. So, what are the warning signs of low trust? Based on research and observations of low-trust cultures, the signs may include the following concerns:

- People are reluctant to take risks or try new ideas.
- Meetings provide for a limited exchange of ideas.
- Most communication occurs in private conversations or via the grapevine.
- People who disagree are cut off, embarrassed, or ignored.
- People have a fear of making mistakes or being embarrassed.
- Some people compete for attention and approval, exchanging secrets and gossip for favoritism.
- People keep mistakes, problems, and concerns to themselves.
- People give minimal effort and do just enough to get by.

So, to improve trust, leaders need to know when the conditions for building trust are challenging. Leaders who are trust builders acknowledge the importance of working to maintain the four Cs. They consistently seek evidence of competence, care, character, and communication.

For Further Reflection

1. How would you describe the trust levels in your school?
2. What indicators from the list of low trust levels might be present?
3. How can your understanding of the four Cs of trust (competence, care, character, and communication) help you facilitate trust in your school?

4. Which of the four Cs are strengths for you? What can you do to improve the areas that may not be strengths?

Remember

The four Cs of trust are competence, care, character, and communication. Information about trust can help school leaders model and maintain trusting relationships.

Listen Actively

Most people do not listen with the intent to understand;
they listen with the intent to reply.

—Stephen Covey

What does it mean to listen actively? Listening is more than the physical act of hearing words. As G. K. Chesterton said, "There's a lot of difference between listening and hearing." Listening is your effort to hear and understand what others are saying. When you listen actively, you understand the total message, including the meaning beyond the spoken words. Listening can be developed, practiced, and refined. When you are a good listener, you help others talk and share their feelings. You help them gain clarity about problems they are having, and you help them find their own answers. When you are a good listener, people want to talk to you.

Good relationships require good communication. The way you respond to others can build trust. When you actively listen to others, you show that you care about them. When you listen carefully, you communicate that you want to understand them. When you are trying to be a good listener, you are saying to the other person: I care, I am trying to understand, what you say is important, and I want to know you and understand what you believe. In this way, good listeners deepen their connections with others.

For most people, being an active listener does not come naturally. In fact, it requires a great deal of effort. The following steps can be used to help develop good listening skills.

1. CONSIDER YOUR INTENTION FOR LISTENING. Effective listeners are genuine in their concern and care for others. They aspire to be supportive and helpful to the speaker. Their intention is to listen in a way that helps the other person gain clarity and feel accepted. Think about it—what is your purpose for listening?

To be an effective listener, you need to come from a place of wanting to hear and wanting to listen. You want to be supportive. Your intention is not to solve or fix or judge. To be a helpful listener, you need to select an environment that is conducive to a conversation, without interruptions or distractions. In addition, a supportive listener comes with an open mind and without judgment. You are open to new ideas. You might have strong opinions, but you put those aside and wait. As a helpful listener, you honor others by assuming that they have their own answers and just need time for those answers to surface.

2. CHECK YOUR NONVERBAL COMMUNICATION. When you are trying to be a supportive listener, you establish eye contact. You sit in a way that allows you and the listener to face each other. You move away from your computer and put down your phone. Your body language communicates, "I want to listen to you." You purposefully ensure that distractions are minimized and that your body language does not imply that you would rather be doing something else, including checking your texts, your e-mails, or the clock. You avoid potential interruptions so that you can focus wholeheartedly on the person you are with at that moment. Checking texts or e-mails when trying to listen sends a clear message that the other person is not as important as whoever else might be trying to reach you. Demonstrating these nonverbal behaviors can be a quick and powerful trust buster.

3. PARAPHRASE. A key to effective listening is paraphrasing. When you paraphrase, you reply with your interpretation of what the other person is saying. You do not repeat his message word for word, but rather the meaning of the message. When you paraphrase, get to the point, and use your own words to reflect what he said, how he felt, and what his words meant. Paraphrasing is very powerful because it allows the person to hear himself and hear how his words can be interpreted, perhaps in a different way than intended. By listening to your paraphrase, he can understand better what he is saying and will often clarify the meaning. You are helping him think out loud and reflect upon what he has said. Often, answers to problems become clearer to others when they can hear their thoughts in someone else's words.

When you are paraphrasing, you are listening for two key ingredients: (1) meaning and (2) feelings. Sometimes the speaker will not express her feelings verbally and will use nonverbal clues such as tone, body language, and word choice to disclose feelings of anger, frustration, relief, excitement, or fear. An example of a paraphrase is: "So, you are feeling angry because your team did not include you?" Pause and let her tell you, "Yes, that's how I feel," or "No, this is how I feel." Likely, she will add more information and clarify what she means. Remember she is talking to hear herself think. Your job is to listen and allow that thinking to happen.

4. ASK CLARIFYING QUESTIONS. These types of questions, such as, "Can you tell me more?" or "What did you mean by . . ." can help the speaker think more deeply about the issue or concern. Clarifying with questions helps you and the other person get more information. When someone believes that the other person understands what she has said *and* how she feels, she often feels affirmed and heard.

5. SUMMARIZE. As your speaker continues, take time to summarize key points or themes you have heard. Sometimes a well-stated summary turns on a light for a solution that the person did not think of before. When people know that they have been heard and that you understand the message by your summarizing, then they will be more willing to listen to you and trust what you say.

Avoid These Listening Habits

In the same way that there are techniques for developing stronger active-listening habits, there are also behaviors that have a negative impact on the listening experience. When you listen to people, avoid these common bad listening techniques:

- Do not say how you handled similar situations or how you would feel in their shoes.
- Do not change the focus back to you. Avoid telling them about the time you had the same problem. Remember, this is not about you.
- Don't try to start giving them resources or solutions unless they ask you for ideas. Active listening does not mean you are there to solve their problems.
- Don't judge them. Statements such as "What were you thinking?" or "That's awful!" imply they did something wrong. Avoid saying whether they are right or wrong. Judgment can increase their fears about sharing and cause them to withdraw.
- Let them finish. It is easy to interrupt or jump in, but these behaviors disrupt the conversation and change the focus of the conversation as well as your role as a listener.
- Be comfortable with silence and pauses. These gaps are healthy; you do not have to fill all the spaces with words.
- Give them your undivided attention. If your mind wanders, grab it and bring it back.
- Do not think about your reply before they have finished talking and had a chance to say what they want to say. This action is interrupting without opening your mouth. Again, your role as the listener has been disrupted, and you are no longer focused on what they are saying or on their need to be heard.

Listening actively is an important component in building a trusting climate. In fact, when you listen actively, trust building is only an "ear" away.

For Further Reflection

1. Who is the best listener that you know?
2. What does that person do?
3. Who are some ineffective listeners? What do they do?
4. Assess your own listening behaviors. What do you do well? How can you improve?

Remember

Effective communication is a key to trusting relationships. Active listening allows you to show concern for others and to support them in solving their own problems.

Be Consistent

Wealth stays with us a little moment if at all:
only our characters are steadfast, not our gold.

—EURIPIDES

G enerally, when we think of consistency, we think of doing exactly the same thing at the same time, and most likely in the same manner. Ralph Waldo Emerson referred to this when he wrote, "A foolish consistency is the hobgoblin of little minds." But, in reality, there are numerous definitions for consistency, such as uniformity or steadfastness. Steadfastness is the best description of what we mean by being consistent as a trust builder, because steadfastness suggests an adherence to the same principles over time. So, to build trust by being consistent, one must have an understanding of one's principles and the willingness and ability to steadfastly uphold these principles. When leaders exhibit a consistent commitment to principles, they build trust in themselves and in the organization.

Instead of thinking of consistency as negative or dull (Oscar Wilde described it as "the last refuge of the unimaginative"), we need to consider the importance of principled consistency, in which trust-building leaders engage on a daily basis. These leaders evaluate their actions on a consistent basis, and this steadfast commitment to identified principles allows them to change their own behaviors or change an inappropriate decision. When leaders make a consistent commitment to principles, they often give voice to an unpopular but ethical need. This consistent commitment to doing what is right enables leaders to advocate for a teacher or for a student who has been wronged and needs support. A demonstration of consistency to principles provides needed strength when a leader moves resources from a popular but low-performing program to another program. These examples highlight the consistency that builds trust.

Effective leaders make consistent, principled decisions many times a day, yet they are rarely described as heroes. In fact, because their decisions might mean that actions regarding policies or strategies previously implemented need to change, these leaders might not be seen as consistent. But, remember, we define consistency as a steadfast commitment to principles. Therefore, these leaders are committed to leading consistently with heart and spirit to see that what is right happens in the school. In the process, they build trust because stakeholders recognize their commitment to being consistent and know they can be relied on to follow-through. Trust-building leaders do not do the same thing every day in the same way, but they can be trusted to be consistent in making decisions that are reflective of their guiding principles.

What can you do to be seen as a consistent trust builder within your school or district? Here are a few ideas:

1. Be reflective. Spend time alone to clearly understand your core values and principles. It is much easier to stand up consistently for principles when you are sure what they are.

2. When you know that a certain action or decision is right, be willing to take creative risks to make it happen.

3. Be consistent in speaking up and speaking out to advocate for those in need.

4. Be consistent in making decisions that are based on the mission of the school. Let this mission be the umbrella under which decisions are made. In this way, faculty members know they can trust you to make decisions that are consistent with the stated values of the organization.

Finally, identify individuals at your school or district who can be part of a reflective support group to encourage you when you need to make decisions consistent with your principles.

For Further Reflection

1. Think of a circumstance at your school that required you to have a consistent commitment to your principles.
2. What supports were in place that helped you be consistent at that time?
3. Describe how you felt when you made a decision consistent with your principles.
4. Identify a circumstance in your organization where you recognized principled consistency in others.
5. Think of a time when you were not consistent with your principles. We know that you cannot undo that deed now (and we don't want you to beat yourself up), but how might things have been different if you had acted with consistency?

Remember

Quietly and consistently, leaders build trust when they steadfastly hold to principles in their actions and decisions.

Use Empathy

Have a heart that never hardens, a temper that never tires,
a touch that never hurts.
—CHARLES DICKENS

Empathy is the ability to understand how others might feel or react in a given situation. In simple terms, to empathize is to walk in another's shoes and to witness his struggle. Leaders demonstrating empathy give of themselves by being present for someone else. The use of empathy facilitates trust building and can deepen the connections you have with others. When a teacher trusts you, generally she believes that you are concerned about her interests and needs. Therefore, empathy is a way that one can build trust.

What does empathy look like and sound like? Empathy can be observed nonverbally in one's facial expressions, gestures, and body language, and verbally in the words and tone communicated. Empathy can also provide a physical sensation in the body when expressed, such as a tug at the heart or an open feeling in the chest. When did you last observe the expression of empathy?

As a leader, if you learn that a faculty member's spouse has lost a job or is seriously ill, you can demonstrate empathy by acknowledging the situation. You might simply say, "I'm sorry to hear about your husband." Sometimes you might add, "If there is a way I can help, let me know." Another example of an event that can invoke empathy is a child getting hurt. Let's say that a first-grade student injures his finger in the classroom door. A teacher would show empathy by considering how slamming a finger in the door hurts, looking the child in the eye, being present, and expressing concern about his finger. She might say, "That really hurts," or use nonverbal communication and hug him. Statements such as "Be more careful," "You should have been sitting down," and "Don't cry" are not examples of empathy. Empathy is not about giving advice or trying to fix a problem. Empathy is being present and understanding how someone might be experiencing a situation.

Being empathetic can help others feel safe and secure in your presence. When others believe that they can share experiences with you without judgment, they are showing that they trust you. They believe that you will be supportive, and when you demonstrate empathy, they leave the interaction feeling accepted, cared for, and even loved. Empathy is a powerful trust builder in that it can reduce feelings of being all alone.

Some experts have claimed that empathy is developed in our formative years, often before the age of five. Still, in most individuals, empathy can be activated and strengthened with attention. Following are some suggestions for developing empathy:

1. IMPROVE YOUR LISTENING SKILLS. Empathy requires you to understand the thoughts and feelings of another. We understand by listening and observing.

2. BE ATTENTIVE IN THE PRESENT MOMENT. Some call this mindfulness, a practice that requires intention and attention to your thoughts. As you become present in the moment, you can become more aware of others' needs and concerns.

3. LEARN FROM OTHERS. Ask your friends and family, "Who is the most empathetic person you know?" How do your friends and family describe empathy? How does it make them feel?

4. CRISES IN LIFE HAPPEN. People get sick, lose their jobs, or experience divorce. Learn what *not* to say during these times. Ask others who have been through these experiences, "Who was particularly comforting to you during this time? What did they say and not say?" Conversely, ask about the words and actions that were hurtful, even if well-intended.

5. PRACTICE SHOWING UP FOR OTHERS. Empathy is about support and attention. Empathy is a gift of your time, your understanding, and your presence. Showing up is a first step in being able to express empathy, as it requires your presence—physical and mental.

6. CHOOSE YOUR WORDS WITH INTENTION. In most situations, we cannot really know how other people feel because we are not in their shoes. So, avoid saying, "I know how you must feel," unless you have experienced the exact situation and can know how someone feels. Instead, consider these slight revisions: "[The situation] must be so difficult" or simply "I care about you."

In addition, empathy depends on your ability to understand your own feelings and needs. If you are focused on how someone's situation makes you feel, you might be reacting from your own experiences and needs and be unable to be present for the other person. In summary, empathy involves a combination of actions and attitudes such as giving, perceiving, observing, listening, expressing, accepting, experiencing, and being present as well as not judging and not giving advice.

For Further Reflection

1. Who is one of the most empathetic people you know? What does she do and say that shows her empathy?

2. Think about the teachers who have the most positive relationships with students. Of these teachers, which demonstrate empathy with students? How do you think that empathy relates to the ability to build rapport?

3. Of the following empathetic actions, which might you improve?
   - perceiving
   - observing

- listening
- expressing
- accepting
- not judging
- not giving advice
- experiencing
- being present

Remember

Empathy helps others feel safe and secure in your presence. Practiced with authenticity, empathy can be essential for building and sustaining trust.

Gauge Your Reactions

*Speak when you are angry and you will make the best speech
you will ever regret.*

—AMBROSE BIERCE

School leaders receive a disproportionate amount of bad news each day at work. New school leaders are often surprised at the amount and intensity of conflict and complaints presented each day. In fact, rookie leaders often comment that college coursework and on-the-job training did not prepare them for the level and intensity of problems they face.

With each problem presented, opportunities exist for building or breaking trust with others. In particular, school leaders interested in building trust consider their responses when dealing with bad news. How one responds when receiving or giving bad news can influence the reactions and motivation levels of others.

When I was training to be a school leader, I had the opportunity to shadow and work closely with six school administrators for an entire school year. I observed five of these six leaders respond with grace under pressure. Each one had developed a poker face and used it when receiving bad news. Even in the most heated situations, these leaders reacted calmly. After listening, they would promise to follow up with the concerned individuals. This response allowed them to consider the situation, gather more information, and respond with care. Consequently, these five administrators were trustworthy and modeled many trust-building behaviors.

One administrator I shadowed showed a very different style. He was reactionary, quick-tempered, and unpredictable. When parents called him to complain about a teacher, he would call the teacher to his office and berate her for the allegations. He mismanaged information so much that teachers constantly were walking on eggshells. Obviously, people did not trust him, and few teachers came to him with their problems.

Most people will lose their tempers on occasion; however, leaders who maintain high levels of trust rarely demonstrate anger flare-ups. High-trust leaders know that many eyes are watching them and will choose their words and reactions carefully. Although leaders can offer apologies when they make mistakes, they understand the power of their words and that they can never take back words spoken in anger.

So how do leaders gauge their reactions and communicate concerns without breaking trust?

1. CONSIDER OTHERS. First, they think about others. What is it like to be in their shoes? What are their challenges and concerns? For example, if a leader needs to communicate a concern about low test scores, she could remember what it was like to be a teacher. What were the challenges she had in her classroom? How would she have wanted to receive bad news about test scores? Leaders concerned about trust think about how they would like to be treated by their supervisors and extend the same considerations to those they serve.

2. ASSUME THE POSITIVE. Leaders delivering bad news generally assume positive intent. Assuming positive intent means that the principal who has to talk with teachers about low test scores will assume that the teachers want their students to do well on these tests. More about assuming positive intent can be found in Trust Builder #9: Assume the Best in Others.

3. TAKE RESPONSIBILITY. When sharing concerns with groups of people, leaders who are concerned about trust will deliver the news with a message that takes ownership and shows that everyone is in this together. By assuming responsibility, leaders who gauge their responses move the group quickly past the blame stage toward a solution and build trust in the process.

4. BREAK THE CYCLE. Leaders concerned about trust do not perpetuate trust-breaking reactions that they have received from their supervisors. For example, a building leader who is scolded harshly by her boss will not pass on the negative reactions to others at the school. Instead, because she is concerned about trust, she will pause, gauge her reaction, cool down, and then consider how to best share the news in a way that will ultimately motivate people.

For Further Reflection

1. As you consider your reactions, how do you handle negative information? How do you handle yourself when you are angry in a work setting?
2. Think about the leaders you have observed. Choose a few leaders whose initial reactions to problems and concerns were calm and composed. Contrast these leaders with those who were quick-tempered. What were the levels of trust with each of these leaders? How did their reactions affect their followers' motivation and morale?

Remember

Leaders concerned about building trust gauge their reactions and monitor their responses to problems. They gain control over themselves and do not speak until they have carefully thought about the consequences of their words.

Use Power Wisely

An honest man can feel no pleasure in the exercise
of power over his fellow citizens.

—THOMAS JEFFERSON

Some have said that power corrupts. At a minimum, the use of power can test character, as noted by Abraham Lincoln, who said, "If you want to test a man's character—give him power." In regard to leadership, the appropriate use of power is related directly to trust: the abuse of power destroys trust, while the correct use of power builds trust. A classic reference for understanding power was provided by French and Raven (1960) more than 50 years ago. They identified seven power bases or categories of power, which divide into two groups: positional power and personal power. Leaders are granted positional power by the nature of their official roles and responsibilities of their positions. Personal power is earned through the use of our personalities or charisma, our relationships and connections, and our knowledge and expertise. Leaders who rely on personal power tend to be more trusted than those who use positional power as a way to gain compliance or enact change. Further, experts recommend limited use of positional power to motivate others.

Leaders have different motivations for wanting to be leaders. Some leaders are attracted to their positions because they want to control others or feel important, sometimes through positional power; however, the best leaders are motivated because they want to use their strengths to help the organization achieve goals. To put it simply, weak leaders use their power to achieve control over others; strong leaders use their power to achieve shared goals. Between these two extremes are leaders with different needs and motivations related to power and control.

Sometimes people are placed in leadership positions beyond their skill levels and competencies. In addition, people might have insecurities about their abilities to lead. Regardless of the reasons, insecure leaders are more likely to abuse their power and focus on the weaknesses of others in an attempt to cover their own tracks. The abuse of power can sometimes be witnessed overtly, but sometimes it might be hidden, known only to those on the receiving end of the abuse. Obvious abusers include bosses who yell, scream, and make unreasonable demands. These bosses might embarrass people in public with criticism and degrading comments.

Undercover abusers tend to manipulate and harass their targets when no one else is looking. These bosses might treat their victims with kindness when there is an audience and then change their behavior immediately in private. Working for the undercover power abuser can be one of the most challenging positions ever, and many experts recommend a quick departure from the job.

Leaders can abuse power in a number of ways. Some leaders use power to control others; others use it to demean people. One common abuse of power is taking credit for others' accomplishments. Abusive leaders create problems with morale and turnover. This happens especially when leaders refuse to relinquish any of their power, as Napoléon Bonaparte did when he wrote, "Power is my mistress . . . I have worked too hard at her conquest to allow anyone to take her away from me." Over time, abusive leaders significantly cost the organization because they can destroy one of the most valuable resources—people.

In contrast, good leaders know that power is a necessary resource for achieving the goals of the organization, and they also know how to use power in appropriate ways, such as empowering others. In fact, Kouzes and Posner (2002) wrote, "We become most powerful when we give our own power away" (p. 285). Wise use of power becomes more about power *with* rather than power *over*.

Consider the following strategies to build trust and use power wisely:

1. GOOD LEADERS ACCEPT THE POWER THAT THEY HAVE. Good leaders do not deny or shy away from power. When leaders avoid using the power given to them by virtue of their position, they create confusion and chaos. Avoiding your positional power can leave people wondering, "Who is really in charge?" Sometimes new leaders are uncomfortable with the authority that comes with their new roles. If they are reluctant to use their positional power in necessary situations, others' confidence and trust in them as leaders will erode.

2. GOOD LEADERS UNDERSTAND THE POWER THAT THEY HAVE. They recognize that power comes from different sources. They understand the differences between positional and personal power bases. Some new leaders, with their lack of experience, rely on positional power. However, the best leaders recognize that positional power is limited and that the best power source comes through relationships and trust building.

3. GOOD LEADERS USE THE POWER THAT THEY HAVE WISELY. Leaders who use power wisely are focused on goals that promote the learning and growth of others. They invest time in developing relationships with others. Over time, staff members who work for these leaders feel valued and tend to be loyal to both the leaders and the organizations.

As a leader, how you use power is up to you. You can use it to help people or hurt people. Remember that denying your power results in others having confusion and insecurity. Sometimes leaders do not know that they are abusing their power. If you are unsure of yourself in your position or believe that you are lacking the skills to do your job, do not try to hide this concern for fear of showing weakness. Instead, recognize your growth areas and find the resources that you need to improve.

For Further Reflection

1. What types of requests or demands do you ask of your employees? Do they believe that these requests are reasonable?

2. How often do you rely on your authority or positional power to get others to do what you need?

3. To what extent are you secure in your abilities as a leader? What additional training or resources might you need to feel confident?

Remember

Leaders who use their power wisely use their positional authority with caution and know that most of their power comes from relationships built on trust.

TRUST BUILDER

Be Transparent

Honesty and transparency make you vulnerable.
Be honest and transparent anyway.

—MOTHER TERESA

Sometimes leaders withhold information or make decisions without explanations. When leaders lack transparency with information or decision making, teachers will fill in the blanks to understand the missing information. They will create theories that transform into rumors, traveling through the grapevine within minutes. The leaders' intentions and motives will be questioned, even in simple matters. Therefore, a lack of transparency causes doubt, introduces fear, and destroys trust.

Being transparent means being candid, open, and frank. When leaders are transparent, their intentions are easy to detect and people are more likely to trust them. Transparent leaders build credibility quickly because of their honesty. Over time, transparent leaders facilitate a culture of collaboration and empowerment. Although being transparent can build trust, it is not an easy ideal to implement when stakes are high or there has been a culture of mistrust. Leaders interested in building trust need to understand the complexities of transparent leadership.

1. TRANSPARENCY WITH INFORMATION. Leaders have access to information from many sources. In organizations where there is high trust, the information flows in all directions. People view information as a resource that can help the organization improve. Moreover, they are not afraid to share information with the leaders or one another. Conversely, leaders share relevant and timely information with their teachers, students, and parents. Transparent leaders are skilled communicators—they do not "overshare" or "undershare." When delivering news, they understand timing and can predict how individuals in their organization will interpret the information. Leaders also understand that they cannot share everything because of confidentiality or other restraints. In these cases, transparent leaders will say, "I can't share all the information right now, but here is what I can tell you."

2. TRANSPARENCY WITH DECISION MAKING. When leaders are transparent, they invite others to be as well. Leaders who practice transparency tend to expect others to be honest and candid. As a result, individuals will offer their suggestions, opinions, and criticisms about the direction of the organization. Transparent leaders value the frequent sharing of ideas and criticisms, knowing that the open exchange of ideas will lead to better decisions. In addition, when transparent leaders make decisions, they explain their reasons for the decisions and the processes they used. When you are transparent, you can build trust because others understand your thoughts. If your thinking processes are consistent, then your teachers will be able to predict your behaviors, and this consistency leads to higher trust levels.

For Further Reflection

1. Think about someone who is a transparent leader. How would you describe his or her transparency?
2. How does this transparent leader share information?
3. How does this transparent leader handle sensitive and confidential information?
4. How does this transparent leader manage decision making?
5. What are some constraints that leaders have in being transparent?

Remember

Being transparent means that you openly share information at appropriate times and that you reveal the reasons for your decisions and actions.

Make Others Feel Comfortable

It seems odd, but observation—not praise, not complaint, not self-deprecation—is the behavior that allows other people to relax in your presence, forget your differences, and enjoy being with you.

—MARTHA BECK

Sometimes your formal position as the leader, whether superintendent, principal, or lead teacher, makes others uncomfortable. Perhaps a new teacher to the school has a problem that needs your expertise. Or maybe the person who just walked into the office is a parent who speaks English with difficulty. Maybe the person sitting in the chair across from your desk is a student who was recently seen for a disciplinary issue. Whether you initiated their visits to your office, or they scheduled them on their own, they are in your office because there are issues to discuss. The success of these conversations depends on the level of trust you have established at your school. One important way you build trust is through your ability to make people feel comfortable in your presence.

Martha Beck, a best-selling author of books on living well, writes that Humphrey Bogart has one of the most memorable lines in all of movie history in *Casablanca* when he says to Ingrid Bergman, "Here's looking at you, kid." Putting this in a school context, Bogart does not put himself down by saying, "Talk to me; I'm just the principal." He does not tell a joke. Instead his comment acknowledges that he is aware of another person's presence and that his focus is on her. The person sitting across from you in your office is a real person. As a leader, you build trust when you set the tone for people to feel comfortable in your presence. You can help others feel comfortable by giving them your attention and removing the attention from yourself, as if to say, "Here's looking at you."

School leaders are busy people, and meeting time is generally limited, so what trust-building strategies help you make people feel comfortable in your presence?

- Be observant; notice if others appear nervous or uncomfortable.
- Set them at ease. Do not begin the meeting with an abrupt, "So, what's the problem?" Instead, I'm reminded of a principal who would begin meetings with a simple question: "How can I help you?"
- Ask questions that indicate your interest in them. In other words, make every effort to connect with them on a professional and personal level.
- Be authentic in order to communicate that you genuinely want to support their requests and needs.

For Further Reflection

1. Have you ever observed a leader who tried to make people feel uncomfortable in his presence? How did this stance impact the trust levels? What were the outcomes of the interactions?

2. As a leader, you already have positional power, so think of situations when you made people feel comfortable who were obviously not at ease in your presence. What did you do that helped to ease the tension? What have you observed others do?

Remember

As a leader, you build trust when you set the tone for people to feel comfortable in your presence and when you remove the focus from yourself and instead direct the focus on them.

Assume the Best in Others

Whatever anybody says or does, assume positive intent.
You will be amazed at how your whole approach to a person
or problem becomes very different.

—Indra Nooyi

Teachers like to work with leaders who believe in them and who trust them to do their jobs. They like bosses who will give them the benefit of the doubt. When faced with problems, they appreciate leaders who will withhold judgment until more information is gathered. One important trust builder is assuming the best in others or assuming positive intent. It means that when you are presented with a potentially negative situation, you consciously choose to believe that people are trying their best and want to do a good job. Assuming positive intent means that you will wait for more information before you react in a negative way. This mind-set can help you become more trustworthy.

Assuming positive intent is a strategy that can help you in many potentially negative situations. When we assume the worst in others, we typically make quick judgments based on limited information. These negative thoughts often lead to anger and frustration. By having this negative mind-set, we start finding reasons to confirm our (sometimes erroneous) conclusions. Consequently, our interactions with others result in conflict and invoke defensiveness; we make little progress toward resolution.

To practice positive intent, one principal considered a problem in his school where teachers were not following the new procedures for reporting truancies. Instead of berating the teachers for being insubordinate or lazy, the principal instead remembered that most of the teachers were hard workers and cared about students, so there must be other reasons for this lack of reporting. He asked questions and discovered that teachers did not understand the reasons for this added task. He was able to remedy the situation by assuming the positive and asking for their help. In most cases, people will go the extra mile to exceed the positive expectations and goodwill that you extend to them.

How can we practice the mind-set of assuming the best in others? Following are two specific situations common to school leaders.

1. DECLINING TEST SCORES. When test scores are lower than desired, you can present these numbers with the assumption that your teachers are doing the very best that they can and that they want their students to be successful. As you discuss the possible reasons with a mind-set of assuming positive intent, you open up the conversation for real solutions because you allow individuals to address the circumstances without having to defend themselves. Their energy is no longer spent on defense and survival.

2. ANGRY AND DISSATISFIED PARENTS. When faced with an angry parent, you can assume that the parent has the positive intention of helping her child. Even though you might not appreciate the way the parent is sharing this intention, you have the potential to de-escalate the situation by holding this assumption in the front of your mind as you listen.

Assuming positive intent is not a typical response pattern in conflict. In conflicts, we can use the strategy of assuming positive intent to start the difficult conversation. Rather than focus on the negative actions that can be addressed later, first focus on the assumed positive intentions of those involved. Misunderstandings and miscommunication are often uncovered.

Although this strategy of assuming positive intent is very powerful in building trust, it cannot be applied 100 percent of the time. Sometimes people disregard and disrespect the basic rights of others, and these behaviors must be addressed directly. Consequently, leaders who build trust understand the need to be discerning when assuming positive intent.

For Further Reflection

1. To what extent do you assume positive intent with your co-workers?
2. What are some challenges for you in assuming positive intent?
3. Think about a problem or a conflict that you are facing. Identify the conflicting points of view. What could be some of the positive intentions of those involved?

Remember

Assuming the best in others is a strategy that will help you build trust. In most cases, people will go the extra mile to exceed the expectation of goodness that you extend to them when you assume positive intent.

Go to the Source

Get your facts first, then you can distort them as you please.

—MARK TWAIN

Going to the source is a common-sense strategy, but sometimes it is not common practice. This one strategy—dealing with the target of concern directly and face-to-face—is so underutilized that using it will set you apart from many leaders. Developing a consistent habit of going to the source will also help you build trust with others.

Going to the source means exactly what it says. When there is a conflict, a problem, or a concern, you go find out more details from those individuals who can give you the most accurate information. Many times, going to the source means directly approaching those who are involved in the situation. Sometimes going to the source means observing the situation and then deciding how to proceed.

This strategy of going to the source might seem so simple—just ask the person directly—but there are many reasons why leaders do not do this. Unfortunately, some assume rumors to be true or take the position that others are guilty until proven innocent. Such a stance does little to build trust. Some leaders avoid potential conflict or difficult conversations with others. These leaders might feel their skills are inadequate to conduct the conversations or be afraid that they will have to take more serious actions. Certainly, many tasks in a principal's job are not pleasant. This role requires courage and good judgment, objectivity, and a commitment to fair treatment for everyone.

At a minimum, going to the source requires courage coupled with good judgment. To use this strategy, one must be objective, withhold judgment, and maintain an open mind until enough information has been gathered. Having the difficult conversations will require empathy. But most of all, this strategy requires courage.

In difficult situations, it is helpful to ask: "How would I want to be treated if the tables were turned?" So, let us turn the tables for a moment. A parent calls your boss at the central office and complains that you are incompetent as a leader. The parent reports that you have failed to meet expectations in general and specifically have allowed students to behave inappropriately at a recent event. In this situation, how would you want your boss to respond? What if your boss decides to involve the superintendent without giving you a chance to share your side of the story? What if your boss assumes this parent's account is what actually happened and calls you to scold you for not being competent? In most cases, people want the opportunity to share their side. They want the person in charge to understand the situation and their decisions.

Sometimes there are legitimate reasons not to go to the source. There might be issues of legality or safety, or a record of continued problems. Yet, at some point, the information has to be shared with the person involved. Most situations can be resolved simply when we go to the source. Many situations become worse because the individuals did not go to the source in the beginning. And many leaders make the mistake of receiving complaints as if they are completely accurate. When asked how a principal could build trust, some teachers have responded in this way: "Don't go behind my back; if you have a concern, just say it to my face."

To build trust with others, go to the source, keeping the following points in mind:

1. Have the courage to seek the truth and go to the source in times of conflict.
2. Check out the facts by asking questions and keeping an open mind.

3. Consider timing when approaching the individuals.

4. Wait until you can have a conversation without being angry. You lose the ability to think and reason clearly when you are angry. Acting when angry can be like driving a car without brakes.

As the leader, you are expected to be able to handle these difficult conversations. When you cannot or will not, you appear to be a coward, and your followers lose respect, faith, and trust in your leadership.

For Further Reflection

1. What is challenging for you when going to the source?
2. Identify a conflict or problem you are facing. Who are the sources of the information you need?
3. When your supervisors are presented with a complaint about you or your school, what could they do to build trust with you?

Remember

Going to the source helps give you the information in the quickest and most reliable form possible. Most people, when the complaint is about them, want the opportunity to share their side.

Delegate Strategically

*The best executive is the one who has sense enough to pick
good men to do what he wants done, and self-restraint enough
to keep from meddling with them while they do it.*

—THEODORE ROOSEVELT

What does it mean to delegate? Technically, delegating is the "sharing or transfer of authority and the associated responsibility, from an employer or superior (who has the right to delegate) to an employee or subordinate" (BusinessDictionary.com, 2012). From a more personal standpoint, delegating means putting your trust in someone else. When a leader delegates, he is putting trust in another—trust that this person can, and will, do the job and do it well. The leader takes a chance that the outcome could be undesirable, or it could be better than he even imagined. A school leader simply does not have time to do it all. Empowering capable employees to help with important responsibilities not only builds trust, but it also allows you to focus your time and energy on the things that are most important to you.

Delegating strategically involves sharing both authority and responsibility with someone else. When you only share the responsibility but do not allow another person to have the authority to implement ideas, the outcomes will likely be less than what was expected. Assigning responsibility to others without also empowering them (i.e., giving them authority) typically indicates a lack of trust on the leader's part. When a leader delegates responsibility without authority, he actually disempowers people—they have more work to do without the faith or freedom from their leader to complete the tasks.

Typically, trust is part of delegation. First, you need to trust others in order to delegate a task or assignment to them. As they complete the assignment, trust is strengthened. Over time, you develop a working relationship based on having the assurance that tasks will be completed and completed well. The following are three key ideas for delegating strategically:

1. CONSIDER FIT. An important part of delegating strategically involves considering the fit—matching the right tasks with the right people at the right time. Effective delegation does not mean you assign tasks to people arbitrarily. Effective or strategic delegation involves reflective thinking and planning. Does this person have the time to get the job done? Perhaps even more importantly, does this individual have the necessary skills? If she does not have the skills for a particular task, then the result will not be favorable. That is why it is critical that you think about what you are delegating and to whom. Considering fit is a key part of strategic delegation, and determining fit requires purposeful planning.

2. PROVIDE DIRECTION. Delegation also requires work and responsibility from the leader to share important facts. Before meeting with people and delegating tasks to them, clarify in your own mind certain facts, such as what you hope the outcome will be and any particulars that should be considered. Then, schedule a time to share these facts: explain the project, due date, and expected outcome, as well as any important background information. If a task is standardized, then take the time to share any rules or requirements. Time is an important fact to consider because delegating tasks at the last minute does not build trust. If delegating a task causes others to have to change personal plans or to put other projects on hold, then delegating is not a positive way to build trust. Added responsibilities that cause people to stay late or rush can actually damage workplace trust.

Similarly, changing the guidelines at the end, after work has already been completed, is also an ineffective way to delegate. Not being specific with facts about what is desired and then being disappointed or dissatisfied when you do not get what you expected is a damaging approach to delegating responsibility. Asking people to redo work because you were not clear in the first place about what was expected erodes trust, doing much more harm than good. This type of inadequate planning and lack of sharing important facts creates extra work for others and for you. Frustration and hard feelings may result, the task may or may not be completed well, and trust is definitely not established or nurtured in the process. Remember you build trust when you think through the facts of the task and share that information clearly.

3. EXTEND FREEDOM WITH FOLLOW-UP. Trust-building leaders who delegate well also extend freedom and provide follow-up. Allow individuals to whom you delegate tasks the freedom to figure out the "how" of the task after the desired outcome has been explained. To begin, ask questions to make sure that they understand the parameters. Some people need lots of freedom in how they accomplish a task; others do better with more direction and less freedom. For long-term projects, plan regular follow-up discussions to check how the project is going. A good leader understands different people's abilities and work styles by considering the following questions: How much direction does this person need? How much freedom should be extended to this individual to complete the task? How much follow-up will be needed for this task? When will the follow-up happen? Will completing this task give the person satisfaction? How much and what kind of recognition does the individual need during the process? Learning to delegate effectively requires the leader to consider fit, provide directions, and extend freedom.

WHERE DO I START? To begin delegating, list the duties, responsibilities, project titles, and activities related to your work environment. Which of these do you most enjoy? Which do you not enjoy? Which tasks could be completed by someone other than you? Consider those people who can help you with tasks associated with your job. As you consider people to help, also think beyond your office staff. Is there someone else who can help? Who has the skills and talent to accomplish the project? Match people's strengths with the potential tasks. When you follow these guidelines, you can build trust by honoring different work styles and matching delegated tasks to individuals' strengths.

For Further Reflection

1. Do you delegate well? How do you know?
2. What are some specific tasks or projects that you can delegate this month?
3. Think about specific employees. What are their strengths? What projects and tasks do you have that match their strengths?
4. Identify a task you need to delegate. Who has strengths to best accomplish this task? What facts and directions about the task should you provide? How much freedom should be extended?

Remember

Delegating means placing your trust in someone else. When a leader delegates, he is trusting that this person can, and will, do the job. Strategic delegation requires giving people the authority, not just the responsibility, to get things accomplished. Remember to consider fit, provide directions, and extend freedom when delegating.

Say Thank You Often

I can live for two months on a good compliment.

—Mark Twain

Think back to the last time someone thanked you for something you did in your job. Maybe she stopped you in the hallway to say thanks for the help with a student. Maybe someone wrote you an e-mail or a note to recognize something you did. How does saying thank you build trust? Being appreciative is evidence that you notice what is right, what is good, and what is positive. Stephen Covey (2004) described trust as a type of emotional bank account that we have with individuals. Some actions result in deposits into our accounts (trust builders), and some actions result in withdrawals from our accounts (trust busters). If trust is like a bank account, then saying thank you is a deposit. Being thankful shows what you value and what you emphasize.

One of the most important points to think about in relation to offering thanks is your attitude. For a thank-you to count as a trust builder, it needs to come from your heart and be sincere. You have to mean it. Your word choice has to be authentic; it has to be something you would really say. Although there are books on how to write a model thank-you note, the way you express yourself—the words you use and the way you put the words together—is unique and characteristic of you.

The use of thank you falls on a continuum. At one end of the continuum is the simple "thanks." At the other end is a specific, meaningful, and individualized thank-you. Again, any sincere offering of thanks can be a trust builder, and with some attention, we can increase the power of offering a thank-you with thought and practice. Offering a genuine thank-you is something we can control. How the offering will be received is beyond our control. Be aware that some individuals prefer to receive their thank-you privately; you can determine preferences by either asking directly or observing reactions of those receiving a thank-you in public. Although the use of public praise can be an effective tool in celebrating the collective efforts of your groups, use caution in offering blanket statements that have little meaning.

Whom do you need to thank? Think about recent activities at work. Who did something worthy of praise? What attitudes or actions did you observe that helped others in the organization? Who made your job easier or more pleasant? Who modeled a key value you hold for your organization? Who demonstrated dedication, responsibility, or charity? Don't forget about those who are quiet, do their jobs, and do not demand your attention. They are steady, consistent, and often great listeners. They bring a sense of calmness to situations. Thank them for being so well-grounded and reliable.

Make a physical list (using pen and paper, your computer, or your cell phone) of these people. Use a few key words: note the situation, attitudes, and specific actions. A list is helpful because many people do not have the time to say thank you at the time they think about it. For example, you might be driving, attending a meeting, or walking around the school. Later you may have forgotten some of the details. By making a list, you can take time at the end of the day or the beginning of the next day to complete the notes.

Perhaps most important, be sure to deliver the message using the method that works best for you. You can schedule a specific time each week to say thank you. You can deliver the thank-you via e-mail, text message, or voice mail right away. You can see the person and say it face-to-face. All these approaches can be effective ways to say thank you. After all, as English writer G. B. Stern pointed out, "Silent gratitude isn't much use to anyone."

For Further Reflection

1. How often do you say thank you? How easy is it for you to think of people to thank? What is a strategy that you can use to increase the specificity or frequency of your appreciation?

2. Whom do you need to thank? Did someone go above and beyond today? Did an individual handle a tense situation with grace?

3. What strategies can you purposefully implement in your daily or weekly routine to make saying thank you a priority?

Remember

Saying thank you is a habit. With practice, it gets stronger and stronger. Saying thank you in a sincere and consistent manner is a great way to build trust.

Communicate Effectively

The real art of communication is not only to say the right thing in the right place, but to leave unsaid the wrong thing at the tempting moment.

—Dorothy Nevill

Leaders who are focused on building trust with others recognize the importance of communication skills. This need to have good communication skills is not a new idea. For example, James Thurber (1961) wrote, "Precision of communication is important, more important than ever, in our era of hair-trigger balances, when a false or misunderstood word may create as much disaster as a sudden thoughtless act" (p. 44). Leaders must consider the variety of tools available for communication. Should one talk in person, telephone, send a letter, use e-mail, or text? Certainly, today's immediate communication tools have the capacity for improving communication in many ways, as these methods can be quick and convenient. These newer modes can improve access to information by reaching a greater number of people. However, electronic media also increase the possibility of immediate *mis*communication.

Even with technology, face-to-face interactions remain the most effective way to communicate. Daniel Goleman (2007) emphasized the importance of face-to-face interaction because it is information-rich. When communicating in person, we combine the verbal message with nonverbal cues such as tone, facial expressions, and body language. In fact, Goleman notes that e-mail, for example, can actually increase the likelihood of miscommunication because it lacks the nuance and rich emotional contexts that are conveyed when we talk with others in person.

Perhaps the most important aspect of good communication is being a caring listener. Leaders build trust when they listen to understand (and not to be understood). Practicing genuine, active listening every day can be one way to build the skill of being a caring listener. (For more information about listening, see Trust Builder #2: Listen Actively.)

So, how do you develop effective communication strategies? We suggest that you begin by following the formula of five Ws: What you say, the Way you say it, When you say it, Why you say it, and Where you say it. These five Ws of wise communication, when they are followed, can result in building trust through effective communication:

1. WHAT YOU COMMUNICATE. Use wisdom and discernment in deciding what you say to others. Many times, as leaders, we say too much and provide far more information than others need to know, which results in the main message being lost or confused. Additionally, we are often too general in asking others to do something. Check to be sure that you have communicated what you intended to communicate. Ask the individual to repeat back what was said, ask questions to be sure the message was understood, provide a timeline, and then follow up. What you communicate can build trust.

2. THE WAY YOU COMMUNICATE. Which communication tool best fits the message you are trying to convey? If you need to send information quickly and the message is clear, then e-mail or texting would be appropriate. If the communication involves decisions, then some type of tool that facilitates discussion is better, such as the telephone, video conferencing, or a face-to-face meeting. Also, the way you communicate involves more than your words. Be aware of your body language when you communicate. Are you making eye contact? What are you doing with your hands? How will the person know you are paying attention? The way you communicate with others can build trust.

3. WHEN YOU COMMUNICATE. When is the best time to communicate the message? If you wait too long, you lose trust because people do not have time to react or respond appropriately. If you communicate too early, people might forget or not take action right away. If the communication might cause an emotional reaction, consider the time of day, such as before school or after school. Leaders who build trust with their communication skills understand the importance of knowing when to communicate with others.

4. WHY YOU COMMUNICATE. Consider why the communication is important. People need information to communicate well with others. They also need information to accept change. Conversely, perhaps you are sharing something that does not need to be shared. Remember to think before you speak. You build trust when you are aware of your purpose in communicating.

5. WHERE YOU COMMUNICATE. The location where you communicate with others is important. If the hallway is busy and crowded, move your private conversation with a teacher to an office. If you are supervising students after school, reschedule a conversation about a student concern with a parent. You build trust when you have important conversations in places that are conducive to listening.

For Further Reflection

1. Think of the last miscommunication that you had with someone or with a group of individuals. Which of the five Ws might have helped you avoid the miscommunication?
2. How can you schedule your day so that you can be more available for others?
3. Assess your listening skills. What can you improve?
4. What strategies do you use to check that others understand what you are saying?

Remember

The five Ws of wise communication, when they are followed, result in building trust through effective communication. Remember the five Ws as a tool to build trust: What
you say, the Way you say it, When you say it, Why you say it,
and Where you say it.

Set High Expectations

High expectations are the key to everything.

—Sam Walton

Leaders who are trust builders understand the need to set high expectations for everyone in the school. That includes the leader. Yes, trust builders set high expectations for everyone, and they begin with themselves. In this way, they model their own challenge to achieve high expectations, and at the same time, they are encouraging high expectations for everyone else. Leaders talk about the expectations they have for themselves as leaders and educators. In fact, an important step in achieving any standard is to let others know what the standard is.

When leaders set and acknowledge their own high expectations, they encourage and support faculty members and staff in setting high expectations for themselves. When faculty members and staff set and acknowledge their high expectations, they encourage and support students in setting high expectations for themselves. Thus, everyone in the school is focused on setting, acknowledging, or meeting high expectations. Often, high expectations result in high achievement. As American inventor Charles F. Kettering, holder of 186 patents, noted, "High achievement always takes place in the framework of high expectation."

How do leaders build trust through setting high standards? An important component when setting high expectations is to provide a foundation for success. In other words, effective, trust-building leaders do not just verbalize their high standards and those of others in the school; they work to set the stage for high standards to be met. Here are some things they do:

- Leaders provide support, such as collaborative scheduling for team members.
- Leaders provide resources.
- Leaders provide encouragement.
- Leaders model high expectations themselves.
- Leaders actively supervise what occurs in their schools.
- Leaders provide feedback and direction for employees who lack competence.

Leaders do not let their fear of not achieving a high standard keep them from aiming high. After all, what if Babe Ruth had never swung the bat because he might miss the ball, or if Thomas Edison had never tried the 100th time to invent the lightbulb, or if the Wright brothers had been content with their bicycles? Michelangelo said, "The greater danger for most of us lies not in setting our aim too high and falling short, but in setting our aim too low and achieving our mark." Leaders build trust when they have the courage to set the bar high and then follow through with providing the support needed so that everyone has the opportunity for their high standards to be met.

Leaders also build trust in the way they handle the times that they fall short of meeting their standards. These experiences are not failure, but can provide the impetus to critically reflect on what was needed to meet that high standard on the next try. Author Zora Neale Hurston reflected on this experience when she wrote: "Mama exhorted her children at every opportunity to 'jump at de sun.' We might not land on the sun, but at least we would get off the ground." Leaders build trust when they set the bar high and do all they can to help everyone meet their high standards.

For Further Reflection

1. What expectations do you hold for yourself?
2. What expectations do you have for your faculty and staff?
3. What expectations do you have for your students?
4. What forums do you provide for yourself, faculty, and students to share the expectations they have set for themselves?
5. What kinds of resources do you provide for these expectations to be met?

Remember

Trust builders set high expectations for others, and they begin with themselves.

Be Visible

Give whatever you are doing and whoever you are with the gift of your attention.

—Jim Rohn

Leadership is a face-to-face exchange, and employees want to see you. In fact, they need to see you in order to trust you. Trust is built on consistent actions. When I trust you, I can predict that your behaviors will be supportive, fair, and caring. Being consistently visible shows that you care and is a way to build trust. Being visible shows what you value and demonstrates your priorities. Visibility is an opportunity to connect with others. When people do not see you, it becomes more challenging for them to connect with you. Motivational writer John C. Maxwell noted the importance of the leader's visibility when he wrote, "Leaders must be close enough to relate to others, but far enough ahead to motivate them."

What times of the day can you establish a consistent practice of being visible? Can you be consistently present before school? During lunches? After school? During passing periods? Make a conscious effort to be visible at predictable times, when both staff and students can count on your presence. That does not mean you will not have days when you cannot be in the cafeteria during lunch or in the hallway between classes, but being visible does mean that people are not surprised when they see you. There is a level of comfort built in to the predictability of your presence and visibility. People know you are part of their day-to-day routine, not just someone who appears when something important is going on.

Visibility as a trust builder is simply walking around your building and making eye contact with teachers and students on a regular basis. Some experts have called this need for leaders to be visible as MBWA, or management by walking around. Regardless of the term, the purpose of the visibility walks is to connect and not to evaluate. Although classroom walk-throughs have become a popular and useful tool for improving student learning, MBWA or visibility walks serve a very different purpose. These walks are, very simply, opportunities to see and be seen. They offer the leader a chance to smile at people, to see what is going on in the building, and to be a part of the daily culture and happenings of the school. Visibility in this way allows the school leader to bond with staff and students in an informal, friendly, and nonthreatening manner.

Being visible is a first step. Building trust involves more than just showing up, but you must first show up to be able to build trust. The following steps can help you establish an effective pattern for being visible at your school.

1. HAVE A ROUTINE. When can you be available: first thing in the morning, right after announcements, during lunches? Review your schedule and find a time that works for you and at which you can be dependable. Also, set a time limit for your visibility walks. If you have an hour to give, give an hour; if you have only fifteen minutes, give fifteen minutes. Regardless of the amount of time available, pick a time that you can realistically expect to make part of your daily routine. Your physical presence will become something that your staff and students expect and rely upon.

2. MAKE EYE CONTACT AND SMILE. Take a few moments to interact and talk about work or nonwork situations. Staff and students feel special when you ask them about what is going on in their lives, and this can go a long way toward building trust. Remember what they say, and follow up on the conversation the next time you see them, because this connection can be a powerful tool for building trust. People who believe that you care about them or are interested in them as a person, not just as employees or students, are much more likely to trust you as a leader.

3. AVOID CRITICISM DURING YOUR VISIBILITY WALKS. If you see concerns that need immediate remedy, take action. But if a concern can wait, make a note and move on. You can follow up with a private meeting to address it at a later date. Using visibility time to be corrective or evaluative can actually be counterproductive to what you are trying to do, which is build trust.

4. PRAISE PURPOSEFULLY. Make notes on paper or electronically if you otherwise might not remember. When you return to your office, take a moment to write a few positive notes or e-mails about what you observed. These notes should be specific and short. For example, you might observe that the students in Mr. Jones' class were very attentive and engaged in the lesson. You might write, "I enjoyed watching how engaged your students were this morning. Thanks for being such a motivating teacher!"

5. FOCUS ON CONNECTING. Employees will feel more comfortable coming back to you later with concerns and questions.

For Further Reflection

1. Assess your current level of visibility at your school. Does your staff expect to see you walking around? Or do they wonder what must be wrong if they see you in the hall or cafeteria?
2. During what parts of the school day can you commit to regularly being visible?
3. How can you make this visibility a pattern?

Remember

Being consistently visible shows that you care and is a way to build trust. Make a habit of being visible, and establish a predictable pattern of being seen.

Manage Your Time

Time is the scarcest resource of the manager; if it is not managed,
nothing else can be managed.

—PETER F. DRUCKER

Henry Ford said, "You can't build a reputation on what you are going to do." Unfortunately, we have all probably worked with people who had great ideas, but never seemed to act on any of them. They were fine people . . . likeable and capable. But somehow, they just couldn't seem to put into action what needed to be accomplished. Certainly some of these individuals might have been just plain lazy. Some might have already been overcommitted. Others might have fallen into the habit of procrastination over the years. These individuals haven't yet learned that, as English actor Christopher Parker said, "procrastination is like a credit card: It's a lot of fun until you get the bill." Regardless of the reasons, we believe that in most cases, when people offer to follow up or put a good thought into action, they have every intention of doing so. Unfortunately, many individuals simply do not know how to manage their time wisely. Leaders who know how to manage their time work smarter, not harder, and they strengthen their ability to build trust. Trust is built upon keeping commitments. When others can count on you to follow through, trust is more likely to occur.

Leaders who manage their time wisely do the following:

1. KEEP A TASK LIST. A task list is useful for many reasons. It brings to mind things you might forget. It allows you to categorize and begin to provide structure to your day. We suggest that you separate what you need to do by having more than one task list, such as one for personal/family issues and one for work-related duties. Be specific. For example, if it is time to begin hiring personnel, under this heading, itemize steps that you will follow. We caution you against overloading your task list; instead create a list of essential tasks that are manageable to complete on that day.

2. PRIORITIZE. Some tasks are simply more important than others. Separate items on your task list into high-, medium-, low-priority items. This helps you focus on the most important issues.

3. STRUCTURE THE DAY. Create a work schedule that provides structure. For example, do not check and respond to e-mail constantly. Set aside a time during the day (or several times during the day) to follow up using this communication tool. Without a schedule, you are likely to never be seen in the school halls, so maintain a schedule for doing so.

4. FOCUS ON PERSONAL AND PROFESSIONAL GOALS. Fill your work schedule with action items that are consistent with your personal and professional goals. Follow Covey's (2004) advice to "keep the end in mind." This keeps you from fragmenting your time and instead allows you to focus on the most important needs of the school.

5. LEARN TO SAY NO. Wise time managers realize they cannot do everything. They learn to say no, kindly but firmly. Being overcommitted and therefore unable to follow through with promises can be a trust buster. Regularly evaluate your commitments to ensure that you are spending your time in the way that most aligns with your values and goals. Summing this up, M. Scott Peck wrote, "Until you value yourself, you won't value your time. Until you value your time, you will not do anything with it."

6. UNDERSTAND THE DIFFERENCE BETWEEN BEING BUSY AND BUSY WORK. Your goal is to be busy doing the needed work of the school. Doing busy work is not a constructive use of your time. Regularly evaluate the tasks on your lists, and consider the extent to which these tasks are aligned with your primary goals.

7. DELEGATE. Items on your task list need not always be completed by you. For example, as you walk the halls a teacher mentions she needs a certain supply item. This request does not mean that you need to get it for her. It means that you write it on your list and delegate to the right person, or perhaps you tell her the process for obtaining the item.

8. REST. Wise time managers know the importance of resting their minds and their bodies on a regular basis. You will never *find* time during the day to do this; you must *make* time, because resting the mind and body reinvigorates and rejuvenates so that you are able to make wiser use of your time.

9. EXERCISE. Often leaders are too busy to exercise, therefore, just as with rest, they must schedule time in the day to exercise in order to stay healthy. One way to incorporate exercise into the workday is to wear a pedometer and set a goal for walking a specific number of steps or miles in and around the building.

Leaders who build trust with others apply these suggestions as they go about completing their tasks. In addition, they are flexible. They understand that the very nature of the school leader's job means that unexpected events will happen. The task list that has been carefully crafted, for example, needs room for important contingencies that occur when least expected. Even more, leaders who are good time managers recognize the value of self-discipline to make the best use of their time as a way to build and maintain trust.

For Further Reflection

1. Consider your work habits. Identify ways that you can make better use of your time.

2. Evaluate a week of task lists. To what extent do the tasks align with your primary goals and values?

3. Create a task list for the day and week, and prioritize activities on the list.

4. Assess the amount of time during the week that you set aside for healthy habits such as rest and exercise. Identify ways that you can build healthy habits into your workday.

Remember

Leaders who know how to manage their time wisely work smarter, not harder, and in the process, they strengthen their ability to build trust.

Maintain Confidentiality

*How can we expect another to keep our secret
if we cannot keep it ourselves?*

—Duc de La Rochefoucauld

Benjamin Franklin once said, "Three can keep a secret if two of them are dead." How well do you keep secrets? As school leaders, others trust us with confidential information. In meetings with students, parents, faculty, other campus administrators, and central office personnel, leaders are expected to keep information confidential that others do not need to know. When teachers come to you to share information in confidence, they do so with the expectation that you will not share this information. One simple way to build trust is to make sure that you are not revealing confidential information to others.

One school year in a growing district, the superintendent mentioned at a leadership meeting the possibility of rezoning school boundaries to accommodate growth. The superintendent reminded everyone at the meeting that this information was not ready for distribution; this zoning change was one of several possibilities. Unfortunately, one of the principals shared this possibility with a teacher. Before the end of the day, many parents were enraged about the proposed zoning change. This breach resulted in a firestorm that required much attention to repair. The principal's lack of judgment resulted in trust being broken on many levels. You have probably witnessed a similar experience in your school district.

As school leaders, students, parents, and faculty members share very personal concerns with us regarding their lives. They trust us to keep this information confidential. Yet the temptation can be great, perhaps because of our human nature, to leak little bits of information when talking with others. Some people feel a sense of power or belonging when they can share secret information with someone else. Some people share confidential information as a way to build a bond with another; however, this strategy backfires and results in destroying trust with many people.

In addition, leaders can share information without words. For example, raising an eyebrow, rolling the eyes, or smiling can provide information about confidential matters. Leaders concerned about building trust must be conscious of what they share and how they respond to questions and comments. Many people are good at reading between the lines. Even without saying it, a leader can express approval or disapproval.

Moreover, by sharing confidential information you may be breaking the law. Individuals' privacy rights are protected by federal and state statutes and professional ethical standards. For example, the Family Educational Rights and Privacy Act (FERPA) is a federal law that governs many educators' actions regarding student confidentiality. Additionally, there are general ethical reasons to protect the privacy of children, families, and individuals with whom we work. (For a great resource, see the National Association of Secondary School Principals' *Ethics for School Administrators* in the reference list.)

So, how do you build trust and develop the ability to maintain confidentiality? Here are some suggestions:

1. Familiarize yourself with FERPA policies. Understand what information is protected by law, and help your teachers understand these safeguards, too.
2. Make a solemn commitment to yourself not to share confidential information.

3. Stay away from a topic that might result in you spilling the beans when conversing with others.

4. When necessary, end the discussion when a confidential topic arises. Practice saying, "I cannot say any more about this subject."

5. Discern the difference between when something should be kept in confidence and when it should be shared. For example, when schools and service agencies work together to meet the needs of children and families in school-linked integrated service efforts, what can be shared? (For more information on this topic, see the Center for Mental Health in Schools' *Confidentiality* in the reference list.)

Finally, do not allow yourself to be drawn into inappropriate conversations. If someone begins to share something that you do not need to know, say so and/or quickly change the subject. Maintaining high standards of confidentiality will help you build trust and be a good role model for other professionals.

For Further Reflection

1. Do you understand the requirements of FERPA? If not, review the requirements.

2. Evaluate your own behavior when sharing confidential information. When did you last say something that should have been kept in confidence? What were the results?

3. If someone shares something with you in confidence, in what way can you support that individual without breaking her confidence?

Remember
As school leaders, students, parents, and faculty members often share very personal concerns with us. They trust us to keep this information confidential. Trust is earned when we keep information confidential.

Build Consensus

If small groups are included in the decision-making process, then they should be allowed to make decisions. If an organization sets up teams and then uses them for purely advisory purposes, it loses the true advantage that a team has: namely, collective wisdom.

—JAMES SUROWIECKI

Making decisions using consensus techniques is another strategy that leaders can use to build trust. Decisions arrived at through consensus have several advantages over decisions that are made by one person or a top-down approach. Because the consensus process involves discussion and consideration of various viewpoints, individuals have a chance to voice concerns before a decision is made. Perspectives that might not have been considered are aired, which can provide direction and adjustments so that major problems are avoided. As a result, decisions tend to be more effective and tend to have more support and backing from everyone. Further, individuals who work in organizations that use consensus decision making report being more satisfied and more productive than those who work in organizations that use a more top-down approach.

Consensus decision making is a process that is supported by trust. School leaders who use consensus demonstrate that they trust others to share in important decisions. They trust that those involved will have the knowledge and abilities to arrive at a good decision. Teachers who participate in consensus demonstrate trust as they share opposing viewpoints and ideas. Genuine consensus decision making is highly dependent upon trusting relationships.

What does genuine consensus decision making look like? Consensus decision making, as opposed to unilateral decision making, is a participatory process of making decisions that involves an inclusive group and strives for general acceptance of the decisions. Consensus is not 100 percent agreement, majority vote, or unanimity. In contrast, consensus results when the group can support the idea or at least agree to live with the decision. In addition, consensus requires that individuals make decisions for the good of the whole group as opposed to their individual needs. When a member gives consent to a decision, this does not mean the option is his first choice, but rather something he can support.

Following are some general guidelines for consensus decision making (Quaker Foundations of Leadership, 1999):

1. The group discusses the issues until multiple concerns and perspectives are uncovered.
2. Everyone uses the skills of active listening.
3. Strategies are used to ensure that all members have a chance to talk.
4. Ideas and solutions belong to the group; individuals do not take credit or blame for ideas or decisions.
5. Differences are resolved using discussion. The facilitator summarizes points of agreement and disagreement. Disagreement indicates a need for more discussion.
6. The facilitator summarizes the discussion and proposes the decision based on discussion. She asks if there are other concerns. Finally, she asks if everyone can support the decision.
7. The decision is recorded, and a plan is devised for implementation of the decision.

Even though the consensus-decision-making process can produce more effective decisions and garner more widespread support, it can be time consuming. Because of the multiple decisions that are made in schools, we suggest that leaders reserve this process for decisions that require the support of a large number of people. Decisions that directly affect teachers should be made with a consensus approach to ensure a positive implementation (e.g., professional development, curriculum, teaching strategies, assessment). Leaders can also use a modified version of consensus decision making by gathering input from everyone and then using the input with a smaller group of representatives from various teams in the school. As long as individuals believe that their voices are heard and that consideration is given to various perspectives, consensus decision making can support the development of trust among the educators in a school.

Leaders need to protect the time of their teachers by making sure that they have the authority to make the decision before involving people in the process. Finally, trust-building leaders understand that there are different types of decisions that require different levels of consensus. They know that some decisions require minimal input and some decisions require much discussion from their teachers, students, and community members. Further, they know that some decisions should be made by them alone. Competent building leaders know how to manage the various types of decisions, and they have the skills to move groups toward consensus and meaningful action. When used appropriately, consensus decision making builds trust.

For Further Reflection

1. Think about a time that you were involved in a decision that used a true consensus-decision-making approach. How did the group arrive at a decision?

2. Think about a recent decision in your organization that was made using a top-down approach. To what extent is the decision being implemented? What are some of the problems that might have been avoided if a consensus process was used?

3. How well would a consensus-decision-making approach work in an organization characterized by low trust? Why?

4. Conduct an Internet search using the phrase "making group decisions." Review a variety of strategies to effectively manage

group discussions. What are three ideas that you can use in your next meeting?

Remember

Consensus decision making is a process that leaders can use to build trust, make better decisions, and increase employee satisfaction.

Acknowledge Interdependence

There is no such thing as a "self-made" man. We are made up of thousands of others. Everyone who has ever done a kind deed for us, or spoken one word of encouragement to us, has entered into the make-up of our character and of our thoughts, as well as our success.

—George Matthew Adams

Leaders who are focused on building trust understand the need to acknowledge and facilitate interdependence among individuals within the school. In fact, researchers have consistently found that the stronger the interdependence among individuals (for example, common goals, common outcomes, interpersonal bonds, and communication), the greater the perception that a group is unified and bonded together (Johnson & Johnson, 2009). In addition, interdependence creates a feeling of group responsibility as individuals work together to encourage one another and facilitate efforts to accomplish similar goals.

The strength of interdependence among faculty members is limited by the trust level of the relationships. It is rare that one individual or department member can successfully contribute to another's knowledge base without building trusting relationships. Consider a student who is struggling. Identifying the nature of the struggle occurs when teachers engage in communicating with others about the needs of the student. By talking with parents, previous teachers, specialists, and administrators and combining this web of knowledge, educators can work together to seek positive solutions. Therefore, leaders must acknowledge and encourage the developing, nurturing, and maintaining of positive interdependence that strengthens relationships among themselves and others in the school.

So, how do you develop positive interdependence behaviors that increase the trust level of the faculty members? Here are some suggestions:

1. Articulate what needs to happen, and provide suggestions for accomplishing the work.
2. Encourage faculty members to give and receive help.
3. Create an environment where faculty members freely exchange resources and information. This can be accomplished in a variety of ways that include providing time for others to explain, elaborate, and summarize ideas.
4. Encourage members of the faculty to work in small groups and to observe one another's efforts. When teachers are able to offer support and feedback, they can help one another.
5. When seeking solutions, discourage groupthink and value creativity by encouraging others to think outside the box. Thank team members for taking risks to share their ideas.
6. Communicate how you are increasing your efforts to achieve. Generally, encouraging others to achieve increases one's own commitment to do so. When others are asked to work harder, leaders need to visibly increase their own efforts also.
7. Encourage faculty members to discuss their effectiveness as a group in working together. Ask faculty, "How might we improve our work as a group?"
8. Encourage networking with educators at other schools and districts.

As leaders acknowledge and facilitate interdependent relationships, they build and strengthen trust in the school.

For Further Reflection

1. Reflect on a past success. Identify the interdependent relationships that manifested themselves to bring about a positive solution.

2. Consider a challenge you are facing today. In what way can your acknowledgement and facilitation of interdependent relationships contribute to a positive outcome?

3. Conduct an Internet search to learn more about groupthink. To what extent does groupthink exist in your organization?

Remember

Leaders must acknowledge and encourage the development and maintenance of positive interdependence that strengthens relationships among others.

Follow Through

*It was character that got us out of bed, commitment that moved us
into action, and discipline that enabled us to follow through.*

—ZIG ZIGLAR

Building trust with people requires leaders to intentionally incorporate follow-through strategies. In other words, they simply do
what they said they would do. Leaders who follow through on what
they say do not rely on such common excuses as "I forgot" or "I've just
been so busy."

Regardless of why we do not follow through on commitments that
we made, when we forget facts, tasks, and requests that are important
to the people we serve, we break trust. Not following through on what
we say we will do causes others to think that we do not listen to them.
Worse, they might think that we do not care or that their requests are
unimportant. They might not express these concerns, but over time,
they stop talking to us about their needs and ideas. In the end, we lose
opportunities to build trust with those we want to serve.

Building trust is about caring and paying attention—caring about
the people we serve and putting that concern into action. Forgetting
to do what we say we will do becomes a major barrier that often masks
our true concern for others.

Leaders who incorporate the trust-building component of follow-
through need to develop discipline that allows them to manage

(and remember) the multitude of big and small details that happen each day.

For example, as a principal walks about the school, staff and teachers might report necessary repairs, safety issues, concerns about students, and supply requests. The leader should write these down. To manage all this information, you might carry a small pad and pencil. You might prefer to use your tablet, phone, or other device to note these needs. Some principals utilize the audio component of a handheld device to take notes. Another way to be sure that you follow through is to ask the teachers to send you reminders; this request places some responsibility on those with the need. Also, keep in mind that it does no good to take notes, whether in writing or using audio, if you fail to *review* them later. Develop the discipline to take notes and then look at them later.

Another strategy for developing good follow-through is to make notes on your calendar. For example, when you visit with a parent (in person or by phone, e-mail, or text), typically you commit to an action. You probably tell the parent that you will check into the issue and report back. Do not let the conversation end there. Instead, specify when you will report back (e.g., in two days, by Wednesday, at the end of the week). Then write on your calendar when you will follow up and report what you have found.

It does not matter if the commitment you have made is to faculty, parents, students, or others in the community; failing to do what you say you will do results in a loss of trust in you as a leader. When you make a commitment to an action, you must have the kind of intentional discipline that says, "I said I would, and I will." When you follow up by doing what you said you would do, you build trust.

For Further Reflection

1. Reflect on a time recently when you failed to do what you said you would do. What could you have done differently to have prevented this from happening? What did you do to restore the trust with whomever it was that you disappointed?
2. What strategies work best for you to help you do what you said you would do?

3. Ask those who are closest to you, who will tell you the truth: "How well do I remember the little things that are important to you?"

Remember

When you make a commitment to do something, you must follow through with actions that say in essence, "I said I would, and I will." When you follow up and keep your word, you build trust.

Empower Others

*The beauty of empowering others is that your own power
is not diminished in the process.*

—Barbara Coloroso

There are many definitions of empowerment, but the one we like best is from Kouzes and Posner (2002), who indicate that empowerment is the act of giving our own power away. Poet-philosopher Noah benShea described empowerment in this way: "My willingness to become less, made her more." Empowering others is never about having *power over*, nor is it about sharing *power with*. Instead, when we empower others, we give them *power to* be creative, take risks, find solutions, and do what needs to be done to help establish a positive climate in the school. When we give others permission to think and act, we build trust.

So, how do you build trust at your school through empowering others? Here are some suggestions:

1. SHARE KNOWLEDGE. If knowledge is power, then sharing that information is a way to empower others.

2. SHARE WITH OTHERS WHAT THEY DO WELL. Then, when tasks or responsibilities are given to them, they might understand you have assigned this task not just because it needed to be completed, but because you had confidence they would do it well (see Trust Builder #12: Say Thank You Often).

3. SHARE THE CREDIT FOR SUCCESSES. Identify others who contributed to the idea or activity and let them know.

4. DO NOT WASTE TIME FINDING FAULT. When an idea does not work or something negative happens at school, don't look for someone to blame. Instead, involve others purposefully in ways to learn from the incident and to restructure for success.

5. INVITE OTHERS TO PARTICIPATE. The whole staff should help determine the vision and goals of the school. Once the vision and related goals are agreed on, communicate this information often to everyone. This provides a clear framework that can guide those making decisions and suggesting ideas to support the work of the school.

6. NURTURE LEADERSHIP AT EVERY LEVEL. Develop mentoring programs and establish continuous, ongoing professional development that provides opportunities for faculty members to share their expertise (see Trust Booster #4: Nurture Leaders).

7. OPENLY SEEK OPPORTUNITIES FOR OTHERS. Help teachers, students, parents, and community stakeholders participate in leadership roles.

8. DO NOT HOVER. Do not become a helicopter leader. Of course, when you empower someone with a task, it is still your responsibility to follow up. But you do not need to monitor so closely that you appear to be standing over the "empowered" individual. Instead, stand aside, not over, and provide support only if it's needed (see Trust Builder #11: Delegate Strategically).

Trust must often be given to others in order to be received. Thus, when your actions indicate that you trust others, the trust level grows in your school. Leaders who empower others by giving them the power to create a more effective school engage in an important trust-building action.

For Further Reflection

1. Identify areas where you have empowered others in your school to grow and use their leadership skills. Which of the listed strategies did you utilize?

2. Identify areas where you have not been willing to empower others in your school. Which of the strategies listed in the previous section might be helpful?

3. Sharing information is one way to empower others. What specific information could help your staff members make better decisions?

4. After you attend district meetings and community events, how do you decide the information that should be shared with others at your school? How can some of this information be empowering to staff members?

Remember

Empowering others is never about *power over*, nor is it about sharing *power with*. Instead, when we empower others, we give them *power to* be creative, take risks, find solutions, and do what needs to be completed to establish a positive climate.

Take Risks

The inability to open up to hope is what blocks trust, and blocked trust is the reason for blighted dreams.

—ELIZABETH GILBERT

Trust involves risks; trust grows when we take risks with others. And risk implies that one might not get the result expected or wanted. As leaders in the trust-building process, we often have to take the lead and make the first move with others. We have to take the risk and show that we are human, that we trust others, and that we can be trusted.

So how do leaders take risks? One important way to take a risk in the workplace is to be open. When leaders are open and authentic with others, most people welcome and respect that level of honesty. In fact, most people will not take advantage of someone being open. Being open can be a risk, but being open can result in greater levels of trust. When leaders are open, they encourage others to reciprocate. Being open means that we share with others our thoughts and feelings within the context of our work. However, openness in the work setting does not mean that one must reveal confidential information or personal details.

Picture a leader you consider to be open and honest in the work setting. Think back to when you first interacted with this person. In what ways was she open with you? Was the process gradual or sudden?

Who made the first move? At what point in the relationship did you know you could trust this person? Today, can you observe this leader in a meeting and know her thoughts or feelings about a subject?

When we have built trust with others, they can predict our reactions most of the time. In general, people take comfort in knowing how we will react and where they stand. When people know and trust us to be open with them about our feelings and beliefs, they will likely feel safe. Our openness allows them to see that they will not be harmed, exploited, or betrayed. As such, our openness encourages them to be more open, too.

Some authors refer to this element of risk as vulnerability. Being vulnerable is taking the risk that people could hurt us, betray us, or let us down as we share our thoughts, beliefs, and goals with them. Quite simply, vulnerability is allowing parts of us to be seen. The writer Gail Sheehy compared taking the risk to be more open and vulnerable to a hardy crustacean losing its shell when she wrote, "With each passage from one stage of human growth to the next we . . . must shed a protective structure. . . . We are left exposed and vulnerable . . . but . . . capable of stretching in ways we hadn't known before." In this way, our very openness or vulnerability encourages our growth and leads to a more trusting environment.

When people do not observe openness in their leader, they may be cautious and suspicious of the leader's motives; this suspicion can breed distrust. When distrust develops, people use energy to protect themselves from potential harm. Likely, they will not share information with the leader because they do not trust that she will care for their interests. This lack of trust means, "I don't want to share something with you that you will use to hurt me later." Consequently, individuals in low-trust organizations have less energy to focus on their job responsibilities.

For many people, taking risks and being open requires great courage. When others are vulnerable with us, this act is the ultimate message of trust. They have learned that we are safe and that we will not use their situations against them. As leaders, we can offer a valuable gift to others when we accept them as they are. Being willing to take risks opens us to a level of vulnerability, and this action is important for building and maintaining trust with our colleagues.

For Further Reflection

1. To what extent do you make the first move in being open with others?
2. Do others in your workplace feel safe taking risks with you as their leader? How do you know?
3. How can you practice taking risks with others?

Remember

Trust grows when we take risks by being open and sharing our thoughts and feelings with others.

Respect Everyone

The basic role of the leader is to foster mutual respect and build a complementary team where each strength is made productive and each weakness made irrelevant.

—STEPHEN COVEY

Respect is earned. Authentic respect cannot be required or demanded of others. Respect is not automatically given because of your position within the organization. Instead, respect is won by how you respond to others and to their needs. Respect implies a feeling of esteem or value for another individual. For example, you might respect someone for his work ethic or his honesty.

Typically, respect is related closely to trust. We trust people whom we respect. For example, when a respected school leader makes a decision with which you do not initially agree, you are more likely to trust the decision because of the respect you have for the leader. That trust then leads to being able to support the decision, which is related to your respect for the leader.

Respectful behaviors make others feel more valued, comfortable, and trusting. I am reminded of the superintendent of a school district who did not speak Spanish, yet the school population was primarily Spanish-speaking families. He began a parent meeting by sharing that he was learning to speak Spanish and then gave a brief greeting in broken Spanish. In this situation, the superintendent was showing respect to a group of people who in the past had voiced concerns about being unwelcome in the community. Leaders who want to build the trust level within their organization know that their actions must reflect respect for everyone.

So, how do you build trust by showing respect for others? Here are some suggestions:

1. THINK OF OTHER PEOPLE FIRST. Author Frederick L. Collins wrote, "There are two types of people—those who come into a room and say, 'Well, here I am!' and those who come in and say, 'Ah, there you are.'" Trust builders care about others and work to find ways to value others.

2. USE ACTIVE-LISTENING SKILLS. Listen carefully when others are speaking.

3. BE SINCERE. Say what you mean and mean what you say.

4. BE KIND. Even when individuals need to be reprimanded, you can be kind.

5. TREAT OTHERS WITH COURTESY AND PATIENCE, EVEN WHEN THEY MIGHT NOT DESERVE IT.

6. DO MORE THAN IS EXPECTED OF YOU. One of my students said that her grandmother gave her the following advice: "Once you know better, you are expected to do better."

7. SPEAK THE TRUTH (WITH LOVE).

8. BE PATIENT. Realize that we all do not learn or perform at the same rate. When possible, provide time for growth.

9. ALLOW PEOPLE TO DISAGREE WITH YOU.

10. ACCEPT YOUR RESPONSIBILITY AS A LEADER IN THE SCHOOL.
Model what you expect others to do.

For Further Reflection

Assess your actions related to respect. Review the ten strategies previously mentioned.

1. Rate yourself on a scale of "Most of the Time/Sometimes/ Rarely" for each of the ten items.
2. Which respect strategy do you implement most often?
3. Which respect strategy do you implement least? Why might this be?
4. The list of ten strategies is not all-inclusive. What other respect strategies could you add to this list to build trust within your school or district?
5. Think of a leader for whom you have respect. What sets this individual apart from others?

Remember

Respect is earned by *how* you respond to others and their needs. Leaders who want to build the trust level within their organization know that their actions must reflect respect for everyone.

Use Humor

A sense of humor . . . is needed armor. Joy in one's heart
and some laughter on one's lips is a sign that the person
down deep has a pretty good grasp of life.

—HUGH SIDEY

Humor is an asset within the learning community and can enhance interactions by improving communication, reducing stress, promoting bonding, stimulating team spirit, and promoting teacher job satisfaction (Hurren, 2006). Humor contributes to mind-body balance, maximizes brain power, enhances creativity, and supports the change process (Morrison, 2008). American author William Arthur Ward emphasized the importance of humor when he wrote: "A well-developed sense of humor is the pole that adds balance to your steps as you walk the tightrope of life."

Unfortunately, the older we become, the more serious we become. In fact, according to researchers Alan and Barbara Pease (2004), the average child laughs 400 times a day, while the average adult laughs only fifteen times a day. Additionally, most humor that encourages laughter has less to do with jokes than it has to do with building relationships. The leader whose goal is to create a school where everyone achieves understands the importance of building and sustaining trust. Consequently, she also understands how laughter contributes to building trust, which can support a healthier school climate.

The purposeful use of positive humor builds trust in the school. Here are suggestions for ways that leaders can implement humor at school:

1. BE LIGHTHEARTED. Make fun of yourself occasionally. In a professional setting, there is never an appropriate time to make fun of others, but there is room for self-deprecating humor. Leaders who can laugh at themselves in the presence of others build trust.

2. RELIEVE STRESS. Use humor when situations are stressful. I am reminded of a principal whose school was deemed academically unacceptable because of low test scores on the state's accountability exams. A month later, he began his first faculty meeting of the year by telling a joke about testing. Despite the gloom, everyone laughed. He then announced, "We can laugh or cry. We choose to laugh and get on with our work to turn around this school."

3. LOOK FOR HUMOR. Take time to review what is happening and to find the humor in situations. Then, assist others in doing so. As author and motivational speaker Allen Klein said, "Humor can alter any situation and help us cope at the very instant we are laughing."

4. BREAK THE ICE. Use humor to clear the air when there are issues of change or concern. Humor opens up increased possibilities for communication, as it leads to further dialogue.

5. APPLAUD RISK TAKERS. Have a "wild-idea" exchange. Encourage out-of-the-box thinking by sharing a few of your own ideas. Many of these ideas will be humorous, and you might be surprised that some of these "far-out" suggestions have real possibilities.

6. AVOID OFFENSIVE HUMOR. Be sure that the use of humor is funny rather than offensive. Never make fun of others.

7. ENCOURAGE YOUR RESIDENT COMEDIANS. Draw on the strengths of others who are funny. Create a "fun committee" composed of individuals who like to laugh and can think of ideas to facilitate laughter at your school.

Unlike W. C. Fields, who said, "Start every day off with a smile and get it over with," we believe that leaders who understand the importance of smiles and humor build trust in the school.

For Further Reflection

1. Reflect on a time when you or someone else used humor during a difficult time. What effect did this have on others or on the situation itself?
2. To what extent is humor part of your daily life?
3. Who are some of the funniest people you know? How can you spend more time with them?
4. Which of the suggestions listed might you try to increase your use of positive humor?

Remember

Humor enhances creativity, facilitates communication, supports the change process, and can facilitate building trust in a school.

Treat Others as You Want to Be Treated

Practicing the Golden Rule is not a sacrifice; it is an investment.

—Anonymous

Leaders who want to build trust within their schools or districts do *not* adhere to the old saying "He who owns the gold, makes the rules." Nor do they adhere to the principle of "Do unto others as others do unto you." Instead, effective leaders build trust when they practice the Golden Rule: "Do unto others as you would have them do unto you."

The Golden Rule is such a universal idea that at least eight religions have a variation of this principle (TeachingValues.com, 2009). Following are various religions' versions of the Golden Rule:

CHRISTIANITY: All things whatsoever ye would that men should do to you, do ye so to them: for this is the law and the prophets.— Matthew 7:1

CONFUCIANISM: Do not do to others what you would not like yourself. Then there will be no resentment against you, either in the family or in the state.—Analects 12:2

BUDDHISM: Hurt not others in ways that you yourself would find hurtful.—Udana-Varga 5,1

HINDUISM: This is the sum of duty; do naught onto others what you would not have them do unto you.—Mahabharata 5,1517

ISLAM: No one of you is a believer until he desires for his brother that which he desires for himself.—Sunnah

JUDAISM: What is hateful to you, do not do to your fellowman. This is the entire Law; all the rest is commentary. —Talmud, Shabbat 3id

TAOISM: Regard your neighbor's gain as your gain, and your neighbor's loss as your own loss.—Tai Shang Kan Yin P'ien

ZOROASTRIANISM: That nature alone is good which refrains from doing another whatsoever is not good for itself.—Dadisten-I-dinik, 94,5

When we treat others as we want to be treated, we build the trust level within the organization because this action acknowledges the value and worth of others—a necessary component of trust. For example, consider the last time that the superintendent announced a decision about a controversial issue. You might have wondered, "Why did he do that?" You might have thought, "I wish he had asked me before he made that decision." Obviously, the superintendent does not need your approval. Sometimes, getting input is time-consuming and impractical. But the truth is, if the superintendent had announced the decision *and* provided additional information, you might have been more likely to trust the decision.

So, the next time you are in the position to announce a controversial decision, treat others as you would like to be treated. In other words, when possible, obtain input from others, and then provide a rationale for the decision that has been made. Treating others as you would like to be treated is a trust builder.

What are some strategies that build trust when you emphasize that you treat others as you would like to be treated? Here are some suggestions to consider:

1. ALWAYS CONSIDER, HOW WOULD I WANT TO BE TREATED? When you, as leader, listen to problems from others, ask yourself how you would want your leader to respond to you. Certainly, you cannot always respond the way the individual wants you to, but by considering the issue from the perspective of the Golden Rule, your leadership can be seen as more trustworthy.

2. CORRECT IN PRIVATE. When giving corrective feedback, think about how you would want to receive negative feedback about your performance. Correct in private. Avoid demeaning language. Focus on the performance and not the person.

3. MODEL RESPECT WITH STUDENTS. Correct a student privately when possible. When this is not possible, always correct in a voice that is respectful and not demeaning. Think about how you would want your family members corrected by an educator.

4. HELP FACULTY PRACTICE USING THE GOLDEN RULE. Remind faculty and staff to use the Golden Rule in their interactions with students and their parents. To apply this principle, teachers need time and practice utilizing the Golden Rule in their own behaviors with their students. Review specific scenarios and ask faculty how they would want to be treated. Then ask them to consider how being treated in this way increases trust.

5. RISE ABOVE BAD BEHAVIOR. Do not allow your interactions with others to be influenced by how you were treated before—especially if it was badly. In other words, repay meanness with kindness. Another's bad behavior is not a justification for your own inappropriate behavior. When others have confidence that you will respond appropriately, the atmosphere of trust grows.

For Further Reflection

1. To what extent do you apply the Golden Rule in your work life? Which of your recent actions or decisions reflected the Golden Rule?

2. Which of your recent actions or decisions did not reflect the Golden Rule? Why? What might have been different if you had considered the Golden Rule?

3. What do you consider to be the benefits of using the Golden Rule as a framework for your leadership behavior?

4. How can the application of the Golden Rule build trust levels in your school?

Remember

When we treat others as we want to be treated, we build trust because we are adding a dimension to leadership that acknowledges the value and worth of others.

TOOL 2: ASSESSMENT FOR TRUST BUILDERS

Consider your actions as a leader. For each trust builder, ask yourself how often you are likely to exhibit that trust competency.	RARELY	SOMETIMES	MOST OF THE TIME
1. I recognize the signs of low-trust environments.			
2. When I listen, I practice paraphrasing to help the person talking to me.			
3. My coworkers can predict what I will do in most situations.			
4. I understand how others might feel or react in a given situation; that helps them feel safe in my presence.			
5. I remain calm when I hear bad news, and I think before I speak.			
6. I understand how my decisions can harm others.			
7. I am open with the reasons for my decisions.			
8. I work to make others feel comfortable in my presence.			
9. I make an effort to assume that others have good intentions.			
10. I go to the source to get the most reliable information I can.			
11. When I delegate I consider fit, provide directions, and extend freedom to get things accomplished.			
12. I make an effort to thank people in a specific way on a daily basis.			
13. I am an effective communicator.			
14. I have high standards for others and myself.			
15. I make a habit of being visible and establishing a predictable pattern of being seen.			
16. I manage my time effectively.			
17. I refrain from sharing confidential information about others.			
18. I use the concepts of consensus building for important decisions in my school.			
19. I encourage faculty members to freely exchange ideas and information.			
20. I keep my word when I agree to do something.			

21. I encourage faculty members to make decisions that improve the school.			
22. I share my thoughts and feelings with others.			
23. My actions demonstrate and foster mutual respect for everyone.			
24. I try to incorporate humor into meetings and events.			
25. I treat others the way I would like to be treated.			

Evaluation

For areas that you marked "sometimes" or "rarely," review the corresponding chapters for strategies that you can implement to improve your trust-building behaviors. Be intentional in implementing strategies to help you build trust at your school.

PART III

Trust Boosters

In this section, we present ten trust boosters. We call these trust boosters because they help a leader who has already established trust in an organization enhance and sustain that trust. Some of these strategies include assessing trust levels, nurturing leadership, and reflecting on personal growth areas.

Assess Trust

Where there is much desire to learn, there of necessity will be much arguing, much writing, many opinions; for opinion in good men is but knowledge in the making.

—John Milton

Getting accurate readings of the trust levels in a school can be particularly challenging for all administrators. Many leaders struggle with getting accurate information outside of their inner circle. For example, people are quick to tell administrators what they want to hear. Moreover, some administrators surround themselves with people who tell them what they want to hear, even if the information is inaccurate. Without accurate information, administrators will have difficulty moving toward the improvement of trust. Knowing how to assess trust is a way that leaders can boost trust in their schools.

One of the most direct ways to assess trust is to ask in the form of an anonymous survey. In the following paragraphs, we will provide specific suggestions for using surveys because the misuse of surveys can destroy trust in organizations.

Generally, surveys should be easy to understand, take less than ten minutes to complete, and be designed to provide useful feedback. When you want to assess the trust levels with a survey, an added benefit might occur. When you ask for others' opinions, you are demonstrating a desire to build trust. You are showing that you want feedback and you are not afraid of the truth.

To use the data from a survey effectively, you need to plan for a high response rate. Without a high response rate, you end up with inconclusive data and a lack of confidence in the conclusions about trust levels and areas for improvement. Sometimes a low response rate indicates that individuals are afraid to respond (so trust is likely a problem). Or a low response rate could indicate that individuals are content and do not see a need to respond. Either way, you do not have enough responses, and the results you do have may not represent how the whole group feels. To increase response rates, consider the following tips:

1. WRITE A WELL-CONSTRUCTED SURVEY. Make sure that each item focuses on only one concept. For example, "the principal keeps her word" is better than "the principal keeps her word and follows through." Questions with a rating scale can provide more information than yes-or-no questions. If you use a rating scale such as 1 to 4, make sure you define what each number represents (for example, 1 = strongly disagree, 2 = disagree, 3 = agree, 4 = strongly agree).

2. ATTEND TO DETAILS. Provide a reason for the survey and a statement of how the results will be used. Allow individuals to remain anonymous, and assure them that their opinions will not be used against them. Don't force individuals to respond if they do not want to. Attending to these details can build trust in the process of assessing trust.

3. CONSIDER RETURN RATES. To increase returns, distribute a paper survey at the end of a meeting. People might be more likely to finish it and turn it in than if you send them an e-mail. Although using an electronic survey system has several advantages, if you are concerned about the trust levels in an organization, we suggest not using an electronic system for this particular task of assessing trust. In lower-trust organizations, individuals might not respond honestly if they believe that administration can track their answers.

4. ASK FOR HELP. Ask someone to collect the surveys, or have a central collection point. Because comments might be handwritten or easily linked to an individual, ask for help in compiling and transcribing the results. If you review the individual responses, you might lose focus with one comment and not see the larger pattern of results.

5. LOOK FOR PATTERNS. When interpreting the results, look for overall patterns. Group items by high agreement rates, low agreement rates, and mixed results. For items with high agreement rates, reflect on how to maintain these positive results. For items with low agreement rates, consider these as growth areas. Some items might have a range of responses and show great variance. Could the question have been misunderstood as it was presented? What additional questions might be asked? Rarely do surveys provide all the answers; they usually lead to more questions.

6. FOLLOW UP. Always thank others for sharing their opinions. Recognize the risks that some of them have taken by being honest. Share copies of the summary of results so that individual answers are not detectable, and explain how you plan to use these. Perhaps you will repeat the survey and look for patterns over time; perhaps you will change something.

Do not show frustration about the results, even if some comments were personal to you. If your feelings are hurt, get the support you need in private. Never use the results as a way to punish or embarrass others for being honest. People will read your reaction and decide how honest they can be in the future. Handling the results in a negative way can backfire and change from a trust booster to a buster.

For Further Reflection

1. What techniques can you use to get reliable information about the trust levels in your school?
2. If you have used surveys to collect information about the climate, morale, or trust among staff, which of the suggested strategies have you used? Which might you want to try?

3. Conduct an Internet search of "faculty trust scales." Review a few measurements used to assess trust in schools. For one faculty trust scale, see the appendix of Megan Tschannen-Moran's book *Trust Matters*.

4. Self-assessments for leaders are provided at the end of each section in this book. To assess trust among your coworkers, use the Leadership Actions Assessment developed by Combs (2004). Insert your name in the blanks for 1–10. In the instructions, provide information about returning the questionnaire.

Remember

Regularly assessing trust levels is an opportunity for boosting trust. By handling the collection of information with care, administrators can get useful feedback for improving trust.

LEADERSHIP ACTIONS ASSESSMENT

Instructions: Please circle the phrase that most accurately portrays my behaviors as a leader in our organization. I will use this information to reflect on my actions and set future goals. Please respond anonymously and return this questionnaire to _____ by ____. Thank you!

1. _____ follows through with commitments.

    Most of the Time   Sometimes   Rarely

2. _____ is ethical.

    Most of the Time   Sometimes   Rarely

3. _____ keeps his or her word.

    Most of the Time   Sometimes   Rarely

4. _____ takes an interest in others as people.

    Most of the Time   Sometimes   Rarely

5. _____ is open to suggestions.

    Most of the Time   Sometimes   Rarely

6. _____ is a competent professional.

    Most of the Time   Sometimes   Rarely

7. _____ is a good listener.

    Most of the Time   Sometimes   Rarely

8. _____ addresses others in a respectful tone.

    Most of the Time   Sometimes   Rarely

9. _____ words match his or her actions.

    Most of the Time   Sometimes   Rarely

10. _____ maintains confidentiality.

    Most of the Time   Sometimes   Rarely

Adapted from Combs (2004).

Talk About Trust

Leading well means forming a crystal clear image of what must happen and communicating that precisely.

—MARTHA BECK

More than likely, developing trust is not a strategy you have heard discussed much in your professional work. Further, the quality of trust is not something that we even think too much about, except when it is missing. Organizations whose members mention trust as a concern tend to have toxic cultures. Without a leader's deliberate intentions to talk about building and sustaining trust, most conversations about trust will occur only when it is a concern and related to low-morale issues.

For school leaders who want to build and sustain trust, talking about trust in the context of professional improvement is a practical strategy to consider. When school leaders take time to facilitate dialogue about trust with their teachers, they are engaging in a form of team development. Talking about trust requires the knowledge of what to discuss, the time to openly dialogue, and the persistence to revisit the topic.

How is talking about trust related to building and sustaining trust? Building trust and boosting the trust level are complex processes and require time. Sometimes, the development of trust happens naturally, but more often the conditions in our schools make trust less likely to happen (e.g., documentation of teacher performance, presence of an "us" versus "them" attitude between teachers and administrators). When a school leader takes time to learn about trust and then lead others in an honest discussion about how to improve relationships in the organization, he demonstrates a value for trust. With patience and persistence, individuals will reflect upon their own trust-boosting behaviors, with the potential of creating a more enjoyable and productive work environment.

What is there to say about trust? Trust is something we all know about already. Discerning trustworthy behaviors in others is an interpersonal skill; it is part of our emotional intelligence. Like our other intelligences, our abilities to discern trust will vary. When talking about trust, you will be leading discussions about trust: what it is, what it is not, how to improve the trust in your organization, and how trust is developing in your organization.

To introduce your intention to discuss trust-building and trust-boosting behaviors with teachers, you should be transparent about why you want to improve trust in your organization. Some teachers might distrust your intention to talk about trust. So, it is important to explain why having an organization characterized by trust matters to you, the teachers, and the students. When discussing trust, you will want to establish ground rules to promote a safe environment for sharing. Depending on the organization's history, individuals might be afraid to share their honest feelings. With consistent, trust-boosting behaviors and time, the lack of trust among staff members will likely improve.

The perfect time to talk about trust is when trust is forming and developing, such as at the beginning of a new year, with new leaders, and with new students. Because developing trust in an organization is an ongoing process involving relationships among the individuals, the discussions should continue over time, allowing you to establish an atmosphere centered on trust. Talking about relationships and trust behaviors can help teams reach new levels of effectiveness. At the same time, the topic can be sensitive and personal for some individuals; learn about your audience and anticipate needs and concerns prior to opening a can of worms.

Leaders should also work with their staff to define trust-busting behaviors. A guiding question could be, "What actions or behaviors lead you to *not* trust people?" Likewise, define trust-building behaviors. In a similar manner, have faculty brainstorm lists of trust-building behaviors through guiding questions such as, "What actions or behaviors encourage you to trust people?" Once an understanding of trust is gained, begin a conversation to discuss how to sustain or boost the trust level in your organization.

With each question posed in the previous section, faculty can divide into groups and work together to develop a master list of these types of behaviors. Revisit and reflect upon the trust-building and trust-boosting behaviors. Do not force discussion of self-reflections, as it could leave teachers feeling vulnerable and unsafe. Maintaining emotional safety and reducing vulnerability are elements of building and boosting trust as you engage in these discussions.

For Further Reflection

1. Have you participated in conversations about trust-building and trust-boosting behaviors with a group of people? If so, was it a positive or negative experience? Why?
2. Predict what your colleagues might describe as trust-building behaviors in your school.
3. Predict what your colleagues might describe as trust-boosting behaviors in your school.

Remember
When school leaders take time to encourage dialogue about trust with their teachers, they share their commitment to building and boosting trust.

TRUST BOOSTER

Recognize Talent

*Of all the things I have done, the most vital is coordinating
the talents of those who work for us and pointing them
towards a certain goal.*

—Walt Disney

As school leaders interested in building and sustaining trust, recognizing talent is a practical strategy to consider. School leaders who recognize talent find the strengths in their staff, teachers, and students and share these strengths with these individuals. Think of yourself as a talent scout—scouts need to know where to look, what to look for, and how to encourage the talent once they find it. Recognizing talent is like being the flashlight that illuminates the good, the positive, and the enduring strengths in others.

Recognizing and acknowledging talent embodies the trust process: First, observing talent takes time, just like building trust does. Second, recognizing talent requires a focus on the other person. Third, sharing with another about her strengths creates a connection. Further, this connection is centered on what is positive and noteworthy. By recognizing the talents in others, you are indirectly revealing what you value, which is another way to be transparent. And transparency, shown over time, is one way to demonstrate your trustworthiness. Of course, with all the strategies for building trust, authenticity is essential. If others perceive you as phoney, these strategies for building and sustaining trust can backfire.

So how do you become better at recognizing talent?

1. LEARN ABOUT NEW TALENTS. If you need to learn more about the talents of being an effective teacher, seek out resources. Beyond teaching, learn about the talents in a few new areas. (Some ideas are leading, speaking, listening, entertaining, analyzing, problem solving, relating to others, etc.)

2. DEVELOP A TALENT VOCABULARY. Think about the talents you possess. List a few of them. Now, take a talent and break it down into components—what are the skills involved? For example, instead of simply saying that you have a talent for organization, think about the specific skills involved in organization. Do you have a place for everything? Do you know what to save and what to throw away? Do you have the ability to project future needs? By being specific about your talents, you build your vocabulary for recognizing talent in others. For more information, learn about the Clifton StrengthsFinder at www.strengths.gallup.com.

3. RECOGNIZE TALENTS IN OTHERS. After you observe talents, point them out verbally and in writing. For example, if a teacher was particularly captivating as a speaker at one of your recent meetings, you could say, "Yesterday when you were talking to the faculty, I noticed how much people enjoyed listening to you. You really seem to have a gift for knowing the right things to say at the right moment." Understand that some people might discount your comments because they do not recognize what they are doing as talent. They might think that because speaking comes easily for them, it is natural and everyone does it that way. Sometimes we have to point out that the skills that seem to come easily are our talents.

4. ENCOURAGE OTHERS TO RECOGNIZE TALENTS. Set aside time in meetings to review specific talents and to allow staff members to recognize talents among coworkers. After the staff members understand talent and have a working vocabulary, you can make this activity a regular routine at the beginning of all meetings. For more information, see the book *How Full Is Your Bucket?* by Tom Rath and Donald O. Clifton or visit strengths.gallup.com/114079/Full-Bucket.aspx.

5. MAKE A LIST. Start with a list of individuals that you would like to recognize. List their names and a few notes about the talents you have observed. Think about what value the talents add to your organization. Then follow through and let them know.

The trust level is maintained and boosted when others in the school are confident that the leader is looking actively for talent and for ways to encourage its growth. These trust-boosting leaders can bring out the best in others.

For Further Reflection

1. Who helped you recognize a talent that you have? How did that recognition influence the direction of your life?
2. How effective is your *talent to discover talent*? How can you improve the skill to recognize talents?
3. List the names of those in your inner circle (e.g., spouse, children, parent). What are a few of their talents? Share these observations as soon as you can; your insight might change the direction of their lives.

> *Remember*
> School leaders boost trust by recognizing talent, developing a vocabulary for talent, and searching for strengths in their teachers and students. Most importantly, they share the recognition of these strengths with these individuals.

Nurture Leaders

*Leaders aren't born they are made. And they are made
just like anything else, through hard work.*

—Vince Lombardi

L eaders who want to boost trust in their schools understand that leadership is needed at every level of the school. In other words, while the principal is the main leader in the school, if he is the only leader there will surely be problems. Leadership must be present at every level. However, it is not enough to recognize the importance of leadership at every level . . . more important, leaders must understand that the individuals at their school have the capacity to fulfill leadership roles when given opportunities. German philosopher Goethe phrased it this way: "If you treat an individual as he is, he will stay as he is, but if you treat him as if he were what he ought to be and could be, he will become what he ought to be and what he could be."

There are leadership roles for staff members, leadership roles for teaching faculty, and leadership roles for students. Leaders boost the trust levels when they implement ways to nurture and encourage leaders to lead at every level of the school.

Before leaders can nurture the leader within others, they must first believe that there is leadership potential in individuals. This potential is often just waiting to be encouraged and developed. So, how do you nurture leadership at every level? Here are several suggestions.

1. SEARCH. Actively look for the spark of leadership. For example, who among your staff goes the extra mile in working with students? If appropriate, you can nurture this leadership capacity by inviting this teacher to lead a staff training session or to organize an after-school activity.

2. DELEGATE STRATEGICALLY. Delegate opportunities to other individuals. You cannot do everything; in fact, you are probably doing far more than you really need to do. Know when and to whom to delegate some of these duties. Be clear about what is expected, and define the final outcome or product. Then provide the person with needed resources (see Trust Builder #11: Delegate Strategically).

3. LET OTHERS LEARN. When you delegate duties to others, remember that you must also back off and give them the freedom to do what needs to be done the way they choose to do it. In other words, they may not accomplish the task in the same way that you would. We all have different styles of leadership. As long as you have defined the final outcome, accept differences in how others choose to get there.

4. MENTOR. Don't let fledgling leaders drown. Even though you must back off to some degree, you still need to keep a watchful eye—in other words, "inspect what you expect." Just be discerning on how and when to intervene. Questions such as "How's it going?" and "How can I be helpful?" allow you to be present without taking control.

Nurturing leaders means that you must maintain open communication so that novice leaders learn and develop how to be better leaders from the experiences you provide. Leaders who are trust boosters work to build the kinds of relationships where they can compliment and critique as needed.

For Further Reflection

1. Who at your school or in your district is a novice leader? What opportunities have you given that person to develop leadership skills?

2. What duties are you currently doing that could and should be delegated to others?

3. What kind of supervision will you provide to a potential leader who is unsure of himself in the role of leader?

4. How will you critique a new leader's completion of a task so that you encourage rather than discourage?

Remember

Leaders who are engaged in maintaining and sustaining trust consider it part of their responsibility to nurture leadership and help individuals become the leaders they were meant to be.

Help Others Deal with Change

Life is pleasant. Death is peaceful.
It's the transition that's troublesome.

—ISAAC ASIMOV

In times of change, relationships and trust are strengthened or weakened. Effective leaders understand how to facilitate change so that at the end of the change, people are still following them. Leaders can boost trust levels during times of change by understanding the change process and helping others move through the stages of change.

Unfortunately, many leaders are impatient with the transition process of others. As a result, they commit several trust busters. When faced with a change, some leaders do not try to understand the thoughts and feelings of others. These leaders might tell everyone to get over it and move forward. They fail to affirm the internal processes that individuals experience during transition. As a result, the outcomes are superficial, and the process destroys trust.

Specific leadership skills that can boost trust during transitions are inquiry, listening, and empathy. By applying these skills, leaders can attempt to understand what others are experiencing. To boost trust, leaders need to address openly the aspects of the transition and accept where individuals are in the process. As a result, individuals can move more quickly into acceptance of the change.

Leaders who want to boost trust during transitions could benefit from the transition model by William Bridges (2001). He outlines the internal processes (emotional, mental, and spiritual) that people experience during a change, into three phases: the ending, the neutral zone, and the beginning. The ending marks the start of the transition process. Something has to end before something new can begin. For example, if you change jobs, the transition begins with at least one ending—announcing your resignation. The entire transition consists of several actions, such as packing your office, saying good-bye, moving into a new office, changing e-mail accounts, and attending orientation. The last phase, or *the beginning*, occurs when you have settled into the change. You might experience the beginning phase at a new job when you are moved in, know your way around, and feel like you belong. Getting to the beginning phase might take a few weeks or several months.

Probably the most difficult and least understood phase is the neutral zone. The neutral zone is the period of time between an ending and a beginning. The neutral zone is marked by contrasting feelings of uncertainty, excitement, anxiety, hopefulness, and insecurity. When in the neutral zone, individuals might feel as if they are wandering around in the dark, going in circles, or exploring uncharted territory. Using the example of a job change, the neutral zone might include the packing stage, the moving stage, the time when you are still getting settled, and the period of orientation, when you have to read policies and ask lots of questions. While in the neutral zone, you might wish you could go back to your last job. You might also be excited by the change and a chance for a fresh start. Being in the neutral zone can be thrilling and scary at the same time.

So how you can use these ideas to boost trust during times of transitions?

1. SHARE THE PROCESS. When a change occurs, share Bridges' process with everyone. Verbalize the endings. Anticipate reactions of sadness and hopefulness.

2. TALK ABOUT THE NEUTRAL ZONE. As people move through the neutral zone of the transition, have patience. Remember your own neutral zone experiences. Listen and affirm others' feelings of uncertainty and excitement. Provide organization and structure for individuals during this time. In addition, communicate to give people the information they need to feel more secure.

3. UNDERSTAND DIFFERENCES. Accept that individuals will move through the process at different speeds. Acknowledge those as they reach the beginning stage. Together, discuss how the transition process can strengthen your relationships. Leaders who understand individual differences during the three phases of transitions can boost trust with others.

In describing the process of managing transitions, Bridges (2009b) writes:

> *Transition* is not just a nice way to say *change*. It is the inner process through which people come to terms with a change, as they let go of the way things used to be and reorient themselves to the way that things are now. In an organization, managing transition means helping people to make that difficult process less painful and disruptive. (para. 2)

Leaders who are alert to the processes and stages of change boost the trust level in their schools.

For Further Reflection

1. What are some changes in your life that you are experiencing or have recently experienced? Identify the ending, neutral zone, and beginning for the changes.
2. Think about a time when you had to accept a change at work (e.g., transfer to a new building, new boss, new program). What was the neutral zone like for you? How did your supervisors support you (or not) during the transition?
3. Review Bridges' quote describing transitions. Select a phrase that has particular relevance for you and describe why.

Remember
Leaders who care about boosting trust learn about and articulate the phases of transitions. They seek to understand individual responses to transitions and to lead the group toward lasting change.

Honor the Past

For last year's words belong to last year's language,
and next year's words await another voice.
And to make an end is to make a beginning.

—T. S. ELIOT

O ften, as new administrators, the past can be a challenge as we move into our new leadership roles. For example, Joe became the principal of a school that had experienced the short tenure of three former principals. The school had survived without an official leader for more than a year, and several of the teachers worked together to manage the daily details. As Joe assumed the responsibilities, many of the teachers were relieved to have a caring and competent leader. Still, Joe was surprised to find great resistance to some of the changes he made in routine procedures. Although he thought that the teachers would welcome his leadership, many teachers questioned his decisions. After Joe reviewed the information about transitions and endings (see Trust Booster #5: Help Others Deal with Change), he realized that he had not allowed the teachers to acknowledge the endings of the past year.

Dealing with the past can be challenging; generally, people do not like endings. In fact, many leaders do not manage organizational endings well because they typically involve a change in relationships and in routines. For a leader concerned with boosting trust, learning to acknowledge the past is essential to bringing closure and then moving forward. Bridges (2001) maintains that before we can really experience a new beginning or a change, we need to acknowledge what has ended.

Leaders who are concerned about trust and relationships will recognize the potential problems inherent in dealing with the past. Sometimes, the resistance to change happens because individuals do not acknowledge what has ended. To boost trust while managing endings, leaders can be facilitators and help others become more accepting of change with a few specific actions: acknowledge the change, ask questions and listen, and accept the stages of transition. The following questions, developed by Bridges (2009a), will facilitate this process:

1. What is changing?
2. After the change, what might be different?
3. Who stands to benefit? What exactly might be gained?
4. Who stands to lose? What exactly might be lost?

Bridges maintains that the first two questions involve the technical details of the changes. When asking yourself and others the first two questions, you are better able to assess the extent to which others understand what is ending. These answers will provide insight into what others value. Listening (without interrupting or arguing) helps show that you care and that you want to understand, which is one component of building trust, and particularly important when dealing with the past. The third and fourth questions help others acknowledge the perceived losses and gains of the change. When people can verbalize these answers, they are often ready to accept the past and move forward.

When listening to the perceived losses, refrain from responding with all the positives about the change. People will think that you are not listening or are impatient. The key to helping people deal with the past is to accept where they are and to listen to their thoughts. Most people move forward when they can make peace with the past.

Joe, the new principal, worked through the four questions, first by himself, and then with others in the school. Because he allowed time to address the teachers' experiences, most teachers accepted the ending of the former leadership regimes and moved forward with the new principal to create a school focused on the students. By acknowledging their previous experiences, the new leader provided a form of validation for past work and opened a path for a new beginning. In so doing, he boosted the trust level at the school.

For Further Reflection

Consider an organizational change that you are experiencing.

1. What is changing?
2. After the change, what might be different?
3. Who stands to benefit? What exactly might be gained?
4. Who stands to lose? What exactly might be lost?
5. If you are a new leader, place yourself in the position of one of the staff members. From her perspective, answer the four questions.

Remember

Do not ignore the past. Although ignoring the past is a common reaction by leaders in times of change, trying to cover the negative feelings and losses will allow them to linger. Give others a chance to consider the past and the impact of the new beginnings.

Allow People to Fail

Failure is only the opportunity to begin again,
only this time more wisely.

—HENRY FORD

Allowing people to fail with dignity and using this failure as a learning tool is a practical way to boost trust. Effective leaders understand the potential of failure to be a building block for success. Identifying a way that won't work, as Thomas Edison said, is an important step to finding a way that will work. In fact, Edison claimed that he did not fail but had "just found 10,000 ways" that didn't work. Leaders boost trust within their school or district when they have the kind of relationships with faculty or students that allow honest assessment of policies and procedures. It is during this time of assessment and critique that leaders can discuss what is not working or what needs to work better, without resorting to blaming others for failure.

People in organizations will rarely take risks of any kind if they fear being blamed if the idea fails. Leaders who blame faculty members for failure are using trust-busting behaviors. In fact, when people fear failure, they might quit trying. On the other hand, leaders who communicate that identifying and accepting failure can actually be helpful encourage others to find a better way. They create a learning culture where there is the freedom to fail, and in this way growth occurs, as they trust individuals to be creative and to brainstorm collaboratively and learn from their mistakes.

So what kinds of behaviors do leaders employ that communicate to others that failure can be a natural and often a necessary step toward success?

1. FOCUS ON LEARNING. When mistakes occur, leaders do not focus on the mistake, but instead provide feedback that is positive and builds toward the future. They ask questions such as: "What could we have done differently? What did we learn from this experience? How can we use that learning to improve our policies, procedures, and even ourselves?" As Covey (2006) wrote, "There is wisdom in recognizing the capacity of people to learn from their mistakes" (p. 117).

2. ASK QUESTIONS. Leaders share openly about their own mistakes. They model how to frame critiques that are focused on solutions rather than blame. In a faculty meeting, perhaps, they address the mistake or the policy/procedure that might not be working. They invite candid critique and use the feedback to improve the situation.

3. ALLOW OTHERS TO KEEP THEIR DIGNITY. Leaders are respectful and discerning. They understand that when others make mistakes, sometimes these discussions should be addressed in private. They refrain from comments that could be embarrassing to individuals involved.

4. FACILITATE DISCUSSIONS AND DEBATES. They engage faculty members in open forums where idea exchanges are wide-ranging. They invite a brainstorming of multiple solutions and a discussion of opposing viewpoints. They demonstrate the group facilitation skills to manage debates in a way that keeps the focus on the issues rather than the individuals.

Being unwilling to play the blame game allows people to fail with grace. In this way, leaders maintain and sustain trusting environments where all experiences lead to greater learning and success. As Benjamin Disraeli explained, "All my successes have been built on my failures."

For Further Reflection

1. Identify a mistake that was made at your school or in your district. What did you learn from this mistake? How were you able to use this learning to improve the school or district?
2. What do you do to encourage others when they have failed at something?
3. Think of a recent personal success that you experienced. What failures contributed to that success?

Remember

Leaders who want to sustain and boost trust within their school or district allow people to fail because failure is a necessary part of the framework of success.

Improve Your Competencies

Be a student so long as you still have something to learn,
and this will mean all your life.

—HENRY L. DOHERTY

Think about a leader or a boss with whom you have worked who was really kind and caring, but could not be depended on to help you with work-related challenges. Although the boss was friendly and likable, you could not trust him to support you. Perhaps he was not able to help you with the technical aspects of your job, he could not get you the needed resources, or he was not available for the real problems. Sometimes these kind leaders will listen with great concern but not follow through with any real action. Although you might like these leaders as people, you probably cannot trust them because they lack a critical component of trust—that of competence.

Competence as an aspect of trust is about being knowledgeable, prepared, and getting things accomplished. Leaders who are not competent might be negligent, apathetic, tired, distracted, or unmotivated. Leaders who lack competence generally do not manage their own resources well (e.g., time, talent, finances, facilities), and they do not manage the incompetence of others well either. Although one can work on the many other aspects of trust, in professional settings, a lack of competence can trump all other aspects of a trusting relationship.

So what do competent school leaders look like? Competent leaders are continuous learners. They have the desire to learn more and to consistently improve their practice. They attend workshops, meetings, webcasts, and other opportunities for professional development. They also share what they have learned and actively work to move ideas into practice. Competent leaders read books, journals, and websites. They are consumers of knowledge in an active, purposeful manner. They ask many questions in order to learn from others. They also learn from experience, taking advantage of things that happen on a daily basis to build their leadership skills. For a competent leader, the desire to learn and improve never stops.

In addition, competent leaders know that they have to interact with the various departments within the school district. They know how to build relationships that will help secure resources and get assistance when these interactions do not work effectively. In short, competent leaders are resourceful and dedicated to ensuring that they have the personal capital to make things happen. Can they get their teachers necessary supplies? Can they ensure that students can access the materials needed to learn? For example, your school might have selected new textbooks or materials for teaching science, but without appropriate supplies, the teachers cannot conduct the activities. A competent leader is aware that the training to use the science equipment is just as important as the availability of the supplies needed to conduct the labs. Therefore, as the leader, you ensure that both types of resources and support are in place.

Competence does require knowledge, but it also requires effort. See yourself as the advocate for the needs of the teachers. An advocate does what it takes to make things happen. Do your teachers know and believe that you are the hardest-working person in the building? Do they trust that you have the interpersonal skills to get the resources they need? Do they believe that you put in 100 percent effort at all times? And, most importantly, are you actively working to improve your skills as a competent leader?

For Further Reflection

1. How do you evaluate your own levels of competence? What methods do you use for learning? How current are you with trends?

2. Do your teachers respect your leadership? Your skills as a manager? Your ability to get things done? Do they count on you? Do they go to someone else?

3. Are you respected for being a hard worker?

4. If you are not organized, what are you doing to improve? Do you have systems and processes in place? Do you actively delegate to those with great competence in these areas? Are you respected in your organization by those outside your building, such as the business manager, human resources, and the curriculum department?

5. Do you get to places on time? Do you participate in a way that shows your interest and your competence?

Remember

Competence involves much more than being caring and kind. Competent leaders have a desire to learn. They are knowledgeable and always seeking to know and do more. They work hard and follow through with their promises. They have the courage to make things happen.

Provide Resources

When every physical and mental resource is focused,
one's power to solve a problem multiplies tremendously.
—NORMAN VINCENT PEALE

Trust boosters seek to maintain and sustain a high trust level in the school. These leaders understand that securing resources is critical to the mission of learning. Resources include good teachers, training, equipment, incentives, and other supports. However, leaders know that resources are not limited to money and things. Some of the most important resources school leaders utilize are the talents and special skills of others.

Leaders acknowledge the importance of developing a network of relationships with personnel in all the other units in the school district and beyond. Effective leaders understand the concept of interdependence and build relationships with the curriculum department, the superintendent's office, and the maintenance staff, to name a few. They know that these relationships are often keys to identifying whom to ask in securing resources and to get assistance when help is needed. For example, teachers might receive various technology resources but lack the knowledge to use or incorporate the technology with learning. A resourceful leader could identify this challenge quickly and acquire the needed support in a timely fashion. Effective leaders see themselves as the advocates for the needs of their teachers and students and have the interpersonal skills to secure resources.

Leaders boost their trust level when faculty, staff, students, and parents know they can trust the leader to not only hold everyone to high standards, but to provide the support needed to attain these goals. Instead of relying on the old adage "Where there's a will, there's a way," trust-boosting leaders acknowledge their responsibility to actively strategize to find that way. So, how do they develop skills needed to provide resources?

1. BUILD RELATIONSHIPS WITH THE COMMUNITY. Network with people within the school community, but also in the larger community. Get to know the parents in your school and their skills. These connections might lead to resources with a simple phone call.

2. SEARCH FOR TALENTS WITHIN YOUR SCHOOL. Talents are resources, too. Find out what hobbies or special skills faculty, staff, and students have.

3. PROTECT TIME FOR LEARNING AND PLANNING. Time is a valuable resource. Schedule the school day in such a way that time is available for learning, teaching, and collaborative planning.

4. IDENTIFY OTHER RESOURCES. Brainstorm with faculty about other possible resources, and find creative ways to use available resources.

5. INTERACT WITH THE MEDIA. Build relationships with people in the media. These relationships can provide a valuable opportunity to communicate positive needs for the school.

Leaders boost trust in their schools by creatively providing resources to assure that learning remains the focus and priority.

For Further Reflection

1. Consider your network of professional and personal relationships. What resources might these individuals provide for your school or district?
2. What is a challenge facing your school or district now? Strategize ways that you can provide necessary resources to meet this challenge.
3. Reflect on resources currently in use. In what ways can these resources be used more efficiently and effectively?

Remember

Trust-boosting leaders know the importance of providing resources. They do not limit their search for resources to money and things but also include people and their talents and special skills.

Engage in Critical Self-Reflection

To be self aware is to be conscious of one's character,
including beliefs, values, qualities, strengths, and limitation.
It is about knowing oneself.

—Philip Burnard

Most leaders acknowledge the importance of learning as much as possible from the experiences that occur in the school. However, the truth is, just because we experience something does not mean we learn from it. Effective leaders reflect on their experiences by debriefing afterward in order to learn and to improve their performance. They ask themselves reflection questions, such as: What happened? What did I do well? What did I not do well? How can I improve next time? Self-reflection can be a powerful tool for leaders concerned with boosting trust.

However, *critical* self-reflection, which takes more time than self-reflection, can be even more powerful because the practice moves beyond simplistic questions about an incident and encourages a person to develop a deeper understanding of herself and others. This deeper understanding occurs when the leader is willing to consider difficult, powerful questions about the event, her role in the event, the relationships, and the outcomes. Examples of critical self-reflection questions include the following: How can this event contribute to my own personal development? How might this experience positively or negatively affect my relationships? What am I willing to do to achieve desired outcomes? How might this experience change who I am and how I am perceived by others? What do I really want to become? Critical self-reflection goes beyond improving one's leadership performance to result in personal and professional transformation. Self-reflection has the capacity to boost the trust level in the school.

Critical self-reflection does not just happen. Instead, trust-boosting leaders intentionally plan and practice how to be critically self-reflective. There are many ways to practice self-reflection, such as setting aside a portion of each day for journaling or introspection. One helpful strategy that we suggest is the ORID process.

The ORID process was developed at the Institute for Cultural Affairs in Canada (Stanfield, 2000) with the intention of helping diverse people work together productively, a necessary component to building trust. The ORID model is simple to use and can be implemented in a variety of ways by groups or by individuals for making thoughtful decisions through reflection. Based on the depth of questions one is willing to investigate, the model is also a valuable tool for leaders to engage in critical self-reflection. For example, the leader would recall an incident that happened during the day and proceed through the following steps, beginning with basic reflection questions and moving to deeper critical-reflection questions:

OBSERVATIONS. The leader considers significant questions related to the event and records answers to these questions. Observations are the facts of what happened. Some examples of questions to solicit observations include: What happened? Who was involved? Why might these individuals have been involved? What caused the event to escalate to the degree it did?

REFLECTIONS. After the leader notes the who and the what of the incident, he identifies the emotions involved. Emotions are often beneath the surface of the facts and sometimes are inferred by tone of voice, facial expressions, and other nonverbal communication.

Questions include: What feelings did I experience during the event and afterward? In what way did I feel empowered or disempowered? What emotions did I observe among those involved? What feelings were expressed? What feelings were not expressed but observed? How might my perception of others' feelings be inaccurate?

INTERPRETATIONS AND INSIGHTS. Once the leader has reflected upon the emotions, he focuses on the thoughts he experienced during and after the incident. For example: What worked and what did not work? What did I learn about others? What did I learn about myself? What were the trust levels among the various people involved? How was trust strengthened or weakened? How do these thoughts provide insights into my personal and professional relationships with others? How do these insights relate to my understanding of how I am viewed in the school?

DECISIONS. Now that the leader has a clearer picture of the incident, has considered feelings associated with the event, and has identified thoughts about the event, he begins to reflect on how he can integrate this experience into his future actions. Questions include: How will I act the next time this occurs? What policies and/or practices must change? Am I more aware of the needs of others in my school? If so, what actions can I implement to meet those needs? What behaviors might I have shown that were trust busters or trust boosters? How have I grown personally and professionally from this event? How will this event impact my life?

Leaders who understand the importance of building and sustaining trust in their schools, their school district, and the larger community strategically plan and practice critical self-reflection. They realize that asking deep and powerful questions will allow them to continue to grow as individuals and as leaders.

For Further Reflection

1. Recall a specific incident that has occurred in your school that offered many challenges for you as a leader. Make notes about the individuals involved and what happened.

2. Using the ORID model, follow each step to reflect about the incident.

   a. What were your *observations* about this event and those involved?

   b. *Reflect* on your feelings and those of others regarding the incident.

   c. *Interpret* the event to identify your thoughts during and after the incident and how trust relationships might have been affected.

   d. What *decisions* will you make as a result of this event and your reflections? What will you do differently in the future?

Remember

Critical self-reflection is even more powerful than self-reflection because it moves beyond simplistic questions about the incident and encourages a deeper understanding of self and others.

TOOL 3: ASSESSMENT FOR TRUST BOOSTERS			
Reflect on your actions as a leader. For each trust booster, ask yourself how often you are likely to exhibit that trust competency to boost and sustain trust.	RARELY	SOMETIMES	MOST OF THE TIME
1. I assess trust levels regularly and use the information carefully to provide useful feedback for improvement.			
2. I engage in dialogue about trust with teachers and others.			
3. I identify strengths in staff members, teachers, and students and share these strengths with these individuals.			
4. I implement ways to nurture and encourage leadership in all areas of the organization.			
5. I seek to understand individual responses to transitions and to lead the group toward lasting change.			
6. I honor the past and provide others the chance to reflect and consider its impact on new beginnings.			
7. I allow people to fail with dignity and use this failure as a learning tool.			
8. I demonstrate my desire to improve consistently by attending workshops, webcasts, and other professional development opportunities.			
9. I seek and secure personnel and equipment so that students can be successful.			
10. I go beyond simple questions about an incident and seek to gain a deeper understanding of myself and others.			

Evaluation

For areas that you marked "sometimes" or "rarely," review the corresponding chapters for strategies that you can implement to sustain trust. Reflect upon what you can do to develop your trust-boosting abilities. Start with a few strategies, and reevaluate your progress each week.

References

Allen, G. L., Peterson, M. A., & Rhodes, G. (2006). Review: Seeking a common Gestalt approach to the perception of faces, objects, and scenes. *American Journal of Psychology, 119*(2), 311–319. doi:10.2307/2044531.

Bridges, W. (2001). *The way of transition: Embracing life's most difficult moments.* Cambridge, MA: Da Capo Books.

Bridges, W. (2009a). The three questions. *Organizations in Transition, 13*(2). Retrieved from http://www.wmbridges.com/articles/article-three_questions.html.

Bridges, W. (2009b). Transitions as the way through. *Organizations in Transition, 14*(3). Retrieved from http://www.wmbridges.com/articles/article-way_through.html.

Bryk, A. S., & Schneider, B. (2002). *Trust in schools: A core resource for improvement.* New York, NY: Russell Sage Foundation.

Center for Mental Health in Schools. (2012). *Confidentiality.* Retrieved from http://smhp.psych.ucla.edu/qf/confid.htm.

Combs, J. P. (2004). Pollution alert. *TEPSA Journal, 68,* 8–13.

Covey, S. R. (2004). *The 7 habits of highly effective people: Powerful lessons in personal change.* New York, NY: Free Press.

Covey, S. M. R. (2006). *The speed of trust.* New York, NY: Free Press.

Family Educational Rights and Privacy Act, 20 U.S.C. § 1232g; 34 CFR Part 99 (1974).

French, J. P. R., Jr., & Raven, B. (1960). The bases of social power. In D. Cartwright & A. Zander (Eds.), *Group dynamics* (pp. 607–623). New York, NY: Harper and Row.

Goleman, D. (2007, October 7). E-mail is easy to write (and to misread). *The New York Times.* Retrieved from http://www.nytimes.com/2007/10/07/jobs/07pre.html?_r=2&oref=slogin.

Hamilton, C. (2001). *Communicating for results* (6th ed.). Belmont, CA: Wadsworth/Thomson Learning.

Hurren, B. (2006). The effects of principals' humor on teachers' job satisfaction. *Educational Studies, 32*(4), 373–385.

Johnson, D. W., & Johnson, R. T. (2009). An educational psychology success story: Social interdependence theory and cooperative learning. *Educational Researcher, 38*(5), 365–379.

Kouzes, J., & Posner, B. (2002). *The leadership challenge* (3rd ed.). San Francisco, CA: Jossey-Bass.

Mayer, J. D., Caruso, D., & Salovey, P. (1999). Emotional intelligence meets traditional standards for an intelligence. *Intelligence, 27,* 267–298.

Morrison, M. K. (2008). *Using humor to maximize learning: The links between positive emotions and education.* Lanham, MD: Rowman and Littlefield Education.

National Association of Secondary School Principals. (2001). *Ethics for school administrators.* Retrieved from http://www.nassp.org/Content. aspx?topic=47104.

Pease, B. & Pease, A. (2004). *The definitive book of body language.* New York, NY: Bantam Dell.

Quaker Foundations of Leadership. (1999). *A comparison of Quaker-based consensus and Robert's Rules of Order.* Richmond, IN: Earlham College.

Stanfield, R. B. (2000). *The art of focused conversation: 100 ways to access group wisdom in the workplace.* Gabriola Island, Canada: New Society Publishers.

TeachingValues.com. (2009). *The Golden Rule.* Retrieved from http://www. teachingvalues.com/goldenrule.html.

Thurber, J. (1961) *Lances and lanterns.* New York, NY: Harper and Brothers.

Tschannen-Moran, M. (2004). *Trust matters: Leadership for successful schools.* San Francisco, CA: Jossey-Bass.